Amagansett Free Library
215 Main St, PO Box 2550
Amagansett, NY 11930
www.amagansettlibrary.org

Photography by Charlie Drevstam

tra.publishing

foreword
5

basics
7

breakfast & brunch
45

small dishes & snacks
81

classics
105

mains
137

sweets & cocktails
187

index
223

foreword

I love eggs. There's something deeply satisfying about dipping a spoon into a warm, soft-boiled egg, with its creamy, runny yolk and tender yet firm white. As odd as it may sound, eggs hold a special place in my life. Whether it's breakfast, lunch, or dinner, they're always a reliable companion.

I've spent countless hours discussing the finer points of cooking them with chefs—the recipe for the perfect béarnaise sauce (shallots or no shallots?), the art of making the perfect omelet (is it about the frying pan or the skill of the cook?), and the challenge of a flawless soufflé. Eggs are a touchpoint for so many people, which inspired me to write a book about them.

It's truly magical how transparent egg whites can be whisked into bright, airy meringues or how an egg yolk can transform into the creamiest sauce with just a bit of whisking and fat. Eggs are among the most versatile ingredients in the kitchen, used across every meal—breakfast, lunch, dinner, dessert—and even in cocktails. You can use the white, the yolk, or the whole egg in endless variations.

For decades—perhaps centuries—many famous chefs have crafted and perfected signature egg dishes, almost as love letters to this ingredient. Some of these dishes are brilliantly simple, using only a handful of ingredients.

New York chef Jean-Georges Vongerichten's signature egg dish—a beautifully hollowed-out eggshell filled with scrambled eggs, whipped cream, and caviar—leaves diners in awe. Danish chef René Redzepi offered a unique experience with his own signature dish, "The Hen and the Egg," where guests cooked their own egg tableside in a cast-iron pan with hay oil and foraged greens, frying it for exactly 3 ½ minutes. At Arzak, in San Sebastián, Spain, eggs are poached in plastic bags for a perfectly round shape.

One of the most iconic egg dishes is Chef Alain Passard's "l'Arpège egg," considered the pinnacle of egg preparation for over thirty years. It's a poached egg yolk served in its shell with a dollop of crème fraîche, sherry vinegar, and a hint of maple syrup. Despite its simplicity, any misstep in cooking or temperature can result in disappointment—like an overcooked, sulfuric, hard-boiled egg.

Eggs can be styled in countless ways: served elegantly, such as a perfectly tempered egg foam with a 63-degree egg, or more simply, like a classic fried egg atop a rustic hash at a local eatery.

It took 4,200 eggs to create this book, and in every dish, the egg plays a crucial role.

BASICS

The saying "to love someone is to know them" is particularly apt when it comes to the egg. The more you understand the makeup and properties of this remarkable ingredient, the better you will be able to cook with it. A note on the recipes: unless specified otherwise, eggs are large, butter is unsalted, and salt is kosher. I recognize that every cook's taste is slightly different so please season to taste.

about eggs

The Hen & the Egg

The number of eggs a hen lays depends on its breed. Some hens lay several eggs daily, while others lay one every other day or even every third day. As hens get older, their egg production naturally decreases. Each egg takes around twenty-four hours to fully develop from the initial egg cell to a complete egg with yolk, white, and shell. Once an egg is laid, the cycle starts again in the hen's oviduct. If you looked inside a hen, you would see a cluster of eggs in different stages of development within the oviduct. Hens can produce both fertilized and unfertilized eggs, and egg color varies by breed. Light-colored hens typically lay white eggs, while other breeds can produce brown, light blue, or green eggs. While this cookbook primarily focuses on chicken eggs, it's important to note that edible eggs can come from a variety of other birds.

How Long Do Eggs Last?

In Europe, it's common to store eggs in the pantry or on the counter at room temperature, though it's also recognized that refrigeration extends the shelf life by up to a month. In the US, eggs require refrigeration because they are washed before being packaged, and are thus stripped of their natural protective coating. It is generally considered safe to leave them out on the counter for up to two hours for a recipe that calls for room-temperature eggs.

    To check the freshness of an egg, place it in a glass of water—a fresh egg will sink to the bottom, while older eggs, which develop larger air pockets over time, will float. In addition, if you ever mix up hard-boiled and raw eggs, you can tell them apart by spinning each one on a flat surface—a hard-boiled egg will spin smoothly, while a raw egg will wobble.

The Structure of an Egg

An egg consists of three main parts: the yolk, the white, and the hard, calcium-rich shell. The yolk's color depends on the hen's diet. Farm-fresh eggs often have deep-yellow yolks because free-range hens eat nutrient-rich plants like nettles and clover. In contrast, hens kept in more confined environments are often fed corn or a specialized feed, which can alter the yolk's hue. Eggs with particularly orange yolks typically come from hens with higher carotene content in their feed. The yolk is rich in nutrients, minerals, vitamins, and fats. Egg whites, on the other hand, are primarily made up of water and protein.

Egg Sizes

Egg size can impact cooking results, as larger or smaller eggs may cook at different rates. Store-bought eggs are classified by size as follows:

· XL: Approximately 63 g or 2.25 ounces
· L: Approximately 56 g or 2 ounces
· M: Approximately 49 g or 1.75 ounces
· S: Approximately 42 g or 1.5 ounces

Young hens usually lay small eggs, while older hens produce larger ones. Larger eggs tend to have thinner shells, while smaller ones have thicker shells. This is because hens use a consistent amount of calcium for all their eggs, regardless of size. Young hens sometimes produce eggs with multiple yolks—a result of their still-developing reproductive systems releasing two yolks at once.

boiled eggs

Boiling an Egg

Boiling the perfect egg can be more challenging than it appears. There is an art to achieving a hard-boiled egg without a green sulfur ring around the yolk or an overly dry center and to mastering the *œuf mollet*, a soft-boiled egg with a set white and a creamy, runny yolk.

Eggs can sometimes feel unpredictable; one day, your breakfast egg is flawless, and the next, it's overcooked. While this variation can be part of the fun, for consistently perfect results, read on:

There are many ways to boil an egg. One common method is to bring the eggs and water to a boil, then remove the pan from heat, cover it, and let the eggs sit in the hot water for 3-15 minutes, depending on your desired firmness. This is worth trying, but for the most reliable results, I recommend the following method:

- **Simmer eggs gently and avoid rapid boiling.** High heat causes the whites to become rubbery, while a gentle simmer yields a smooth, tender white around a perfectly cooked yolk. If your yolk has a green ring and a sulfurous taste, it's likely due to excessive heat or overcooking. That's why hard-boiled eggs should be removed from the heat as soon as they're done.
- **Begin with simmering water.** After testing multiple approaches, the most reliable method is to lower eggs gently into simmering water with a slotted spoon. This allows you to track the cooking time precisely to prevent overcooking.
- **Use room-temperature eggs.** Placing cold eggs directly from the refrigerator into hot water can cause the shells to crack. If your eggs are cold, let them sit in warm tap water for 3-5 minutes to bring them to room temperature before cooking.

Peeling a Boiled Egg

If your boiled eggs are difficult to peel, they might simply be too fresh. This can be especially problematic when you're preparing eggs for buffets or gatherings where presentation is key. To make peeling easier, immediately place the eggs in an ice bath after boiling.

There are several other techniques to simplify the peeling process. Some suggest adding baking soda to the boiling water to raise the pH level, which can make the shell easier to remove. Another method is to gently roll the egg on a hard surface, which loosens the shell and helps it come off more easily. For a more involved approach, place the egg in a jar of cold water and shake it vigorously. This will usually loosen the shell entirely, though it may be more effort than you'd want to put in for a quick breakfast.

3- to 11-Minute Eggs: Boiling Times

3 minutes
White is still liquid, and the yolk is completely runny.
Perfect for emulsions that need extra creaminess.

4 minutes
White is slightly firmer but still soft, with a runny yolk.
Ideal for adding a creamy texture to pasta dishes.

5 minutes
White begins to set, while the yolk remains runny.
The ultimate "egg soldier" egg (page 59), perfect for dipping toast sticks.

6 minutes
White is firm, and the yolk is runny with a creamy ring around it.
Considered by many to be the best breakfast egg.

7 minutes
White is firm, and the yolk is creamy-runny. A good middle ground for
those who like a set white but don't want the yolk to taste raw.

8 minutes
White is firm, and the yolk is firm yet still creamy.
The perfect hard-boiled egg with a firm yolk that isn't dry or chalky.

9 minutes
White is firm, and the yolk is firm with a lighter yellow color.
Ideal for egg salads or chopped eggs for dishes like herring and brown butter.

10 minutes
Almost fully hard-boiled, with an almost completely pale yellow yolk.

11 minutes
Fully hard-boiled, with a light yellow yolk.
Boiling the egg any longer will result in a dry, powdery yolk.

fried eggs

Frying an Egg

A fried egg can be served either "sunny-side up" (fried on one side) or flipped. The yolk can be runny ("over easy") or firm ("over hard"). This is a matter of preference, and there are several schools of thought.

According to the classic French technique, the egg should be fried without any browning or bubbles. The white should be smooth and fully set, and the yolk should remain runny and shiny yellow. To achieve this, fry the egg over low heat. To prevent the egg from spreading too much in the pan, use a fresh egg. The white will stay soft and delicate without developing any browned butter flavor due to the low temperature. If you want to further ensure the egg doesn't brown or taste like browned butter, use clarified butter or a neutral oil like canola or sunflower.

Another popular style is the butter-fried egg, where the white takes on a light golden-brown color and crispy edges, and the yolk can be runny or firm. In my opinion, this is one of the most delicious methods, especially when served with caviar, butter, and Swedish crispbread.

The Japanese or Asian version requires more intense cooking. A very hot pan causes the egg to sizzle and jump as it hits the oil, resulting in a fried egg with crispy, bubbly brown edges. This type of egg is great in noodle dishes, sliced in salads, or served on top of bibimbap.

Frying Pan Choice

One of the most important factors when frying eggs, making omelets, or scrambling eggs is choosing the right frying pan. The protein-rich egg can either turn into a beautifully smooth omelet that slides out of the pan effortlessly, or it can become a messy disaster if it sticks.

Many chefs have a dedicated egg-frying pan that's not used for anything else and is seasoned with a natural layer of fat. As the pan is only ever used for eggs, it's never exposed to excessive heat, as it might if it were used for frying meat, which can burn the pan's coating and require scrubbing with steel wool—a method that ruins the natural fat coating.

The best option is a classic French frying pan with slightly high sides, either made of carbon steel or with a nonstick coating. A carbon steel pan needs to be used several times to build up a good surface and natural fat coating. If properly cared for and used only for eggs, it can become the dream pan for omelet enthusiasts. (Note: carbon steel pans are similar to cast iron but lighter and quicker to heat, making them excellent for frying eggs and delicate cooking tasks.) Alternatively, a pan with a nonstick coating works well and makes things easier since it always has a protective layer to prevent sticking. However, be careful not to overheat a nonstick pan, as it will damage the coating and compromise its functionality.

Yes, I have a special pan just for eggs: I usually use a French frying pan with a nonstick coating for making omelets and scrambled eggs. A pan with a coating might be considered "cheating" by classically trained French chefs, but for consistent results, I go with the sure option.

classic french fried egg

Makes 1

1 tablespoon butter or neutral oil • 1 egg • salt • freshly ground black pepper

1. Melt butter or heat oil in a frying pan over medium heat. Crack the egg into the pan and lower the heat.
2. Let the egg cook on low heat until the white is set but still has a slightly soft film on top.
3. Season to taste with salt and pepper.
4. You can serve the egg now or flip it for "sunny-side down" or "over easy." If you flip, fry for about 1 minute on the other side. (A flipped French egg should not have any browned color on the surface. A classic French egg should be entirely white, without browned edges or bubbles in the white.)

butter-fried egg

Melt butter in a frying pan over medium heat. Allow it to bubble and brown slightly. Crack the egg into the pan. Fry until the white is set but still has a slightly soft surface. It should have a golden-brown bottom and the rich flavor of browned butter.

Makes 1

1–2 tablespoons butter • 1 egg

basics

crispy fried egg

1. Heat a frying pan over medium-high heat. Once hot, pour in the oil.
2. Crack the egg into the hot pan. The egg should "jump" from the heat and start to bubble. Fry until the white is set and has a crispy, golden-brown bottom.
3. Season to taste with salt.

Makes 1

2 tablespoons neutral oil • 1 egg • salt

poached eggs

Poaching an Egg

Many people find poaching eggs challenging, and it can be until you master the technique. One common approach is to create a whirlpool of simmering water before dropping in the egg. While this helps the white wrap neatly around the yolk, it often ends in failure—producing separated whites and yolks with wispy strands floating in the water, which is far from ideal. (A word to the wise: an egg-poaching pan makes this process a snap.)

The key to a well-poached egg is using fresh eggs. If your eggs aren't fresh, try straining them by cracking the egg into a slotted spoon and allowing the watery part of the white to drain away, leaving behind the firmer portion.

For the cooking water, it should be simmering, not boiling, with a splash of white vinegar added to help the egg bind quickly when it reacts with the acid. Be careful with the amount of vinegar, though—too much can make the egg white rubbery. If you're preparing brunch for a crowd and need to poach multiple eggs (such as for serving eggs Benedict to a crowd), consider the "rookie method." With this technique, crack the eggs into a vinegar bath (equal parts water and white vinegar) and make sure they're fully submerged for up to 10 minutes before cooking them. When the eggs are placed in the acidic vinegar water, they react by tightening up, forming a round shape. By the time they hit the simmering water, they're already neatly enclosed. While you may compromise slightly on texture—the whites may turn out slightly firm—you'll get beautifully shaped poached eggs without the hassle, making it a stress-free solution for poaching up to 15 eggs at once. This method also works for quail eggs.

Poached eggs can be prepared a day in advance and stored in the refrigerator. To serve, simply reheat the eggs by dipping them in simmering water for no more than 30 seconds.

Oeufs en Meurette (Eggs Poached in Red Wine)

This French technique provides one of the most flavorful ways to prepare poached eggs. The egg is simmered in a red wine sauce along with vegetables and is traditionally served with pork belly, mushrooms, and onions. It's similar to *bœuf bourguignon* but swaps the beef for a delicate poached egg.

classic poached eggs

1. In a saucepan, bring 4 cups (1 l) water to a boil. Add 1 tablespoon vinegar and 1 ½ teaspoons salt.

2. Reduce the heat to a simmer. Crack one egg at a time into a small bowl, then gently tip the egg into the simmering water. You can poach multiple eggs simultaneously, but make sure to keep track of the order they were added. While eggs cook, prepare a bowl of ice water.

3. After exactly 3 minutes, the eggs are ready, with a set but soft white and a runny yolk inside. Remove the eggs with a slotted spoon and place them in the ice water to stop them from cooking further. Trim any loose white for a rounder egg.

Makes 4

1 tablespoon white vinegar • 1 ½ teaspoons salt • 4 eggs

rookie poached eggs

Makes 4

½ cup white vinegar • 1 ½ teaspoons salt • 4 eggs

1. In a medium bowl, combine ½ cup (120 ml) vinegar with ½ cup (120 ml) water.
2. In a saucepan, bring 4 cups (1 l) water to a boil. Add 1 ½ teaspoons of salt.
3. Crack one egg at a time into the vinegar-water mixture, waiting about 30 seconds in between so each egg has time to react to the acid. Let sit for 5 minutes.
4. Pour the eggs and liquid into the boiling water.
5. The water should now be simmering; reduce the heat if necessary. Simmer the eggs for exactly 3 minutes. While the eggs cook, prepare a bowl of ice water.
6. Remove the eggs with a slotted spoon and place them in the ice water to stop them from cooking further.

basics

poached quail eggs

Follow Rookie Poached Eggs directions on page 19, with two changes.

1. Poke the quail eggshells with a small paring knife to crack them open.
2. Reduce cooking time to 1 minute.

Makes 8

½ cup white vinegar • 1 ½ teaspoons salt • 8 quail eggs

scrambled eggs

There's nothing worse than dry, grainy, or spongy scrambled eggs. Scrambled eggs should be creamy, which is why they're called a "scramble" and not an "omelet."

There are various techniques for making scrambled eggs, each resulting in a different texture. You can cook them in a frying pan to form "curds" or use a water bath (bain-marie) to create a smoother, almost custard-like consistency. (If you don't want the hassle of setting up a water bath, you can achieve a similar effect by whisking the eggs on low heat in a saucepan.) Both styles are delicious and have different uses: frying pan eggs are ideal for serving on toast since they hold their shape, while the water bath method results in a softer texture that is perfect on its own, perhaps topped with freshly grated truffle or Parmesan.

You can prepare scrambled eggs with or without cream, but adding a splash of cream along with the butter makes them extra luxurious.

Regardless of your preferred method, low heat is key. Cooking over low heat prevents the eggs from setting too quickly and ensures a soft, velvety texture. Scrambled eggs should always be made à la minute (cooked just before serving) to guarantee they're warm and creamy when they reach the table.

Truffle Scrambled Eggs

An eggshell has about 10,000 tiny pores, allowing the egg to "breathe." This means it can absorb strong aromas from nearby foods. To avoid unwanted flavors, keep eggs away from pungent foods. Or, in some cases, you may want that effect: for example, storing eggs with fresh truffles for a few days will infuse the eggs with truffle aroma, resulting in a delicately-flavored scrambled egg.

Scrambled Egg Additions

Try adding any of these ingredients to elevate your scrambled eggs: dill, Västerbotten cheese,* sesame seeds, truffle, Parmesan, chèvre, cumin seeds, Tabasco, caramelized onions, curry, minced jalapeño, red pepper flakes, fresh cilantro, chopped fresh herbs, chives, or horseradish.

Tip: One of the best toppings for scrambled eggs is dukkah: combine ¼ cup (35 g) toasted sesame seeds, ½ cup (75 g) toasted chopped hazelnuts, 1 ½ teaspoons toasted cumin seeds, 1 ½ teaspoons toasted fennel seeds, and 1 ½ teaspoons toasted coriander seeds in a blender or mortar and pestle. Grind until the mixture resembles coarse sprinkles. This versatile topping enhances not only scrambled eggs but also avocado toast, soups, and pasta.

---

* *Västerbotten cheese (Västerbottensost) is a Swedish hard cheese known for its sharp, tangy flavor and crumbly texture, often compared to Parmesan or aged cheddar. It's made from cow's milk and has a rich, complex taste with a slight nuttiness and bitterness. The cheese is traditionally produced in the Västerbotten region of northern Sweden and is aged for at least 14 months. It is commonly used in Swedish cuisine, especially in pies (like Västerbottenpaj), gratins, and as a topping for various dishes. It's also popular on festive occasions such as Midsummer and Christmas.*

basics

scrambled eggs in a frying pan

1. In a medium bowl, beat the eggs and cream together.
2. Heat a frying pan over medium heat and melt the butter.
3. Pour in the egg mixture. Reduce heat to low, and stir slowly until the scramble forms large curds. Once the scramble is fluffy but still creamy, cook for just a couple more seconds, then transfer to a plate.
4. Season to taste with salt and pepper.

Makes 2 servings

4 eggs • 3 tablespoons heavy cream •
2 tablespoons butter • salt •
freshly ground black pepper

scrambled eggs cooked over a water bath

Makes 2 servings

4 eggs • 3 tablespoons heavy cream •
3 tablespoons butter, at room temperature, divided •
salt • freshly ground black pepper

1. In a saucepan, bring an inch of water to a simmer, and place a stainless-steel bowl or heatproof glass bowl just above the water's surface. Crack in the eggs and add the cream.

2. Whisk continually over the simmering water until creamy and scrambled; this will take some time.

3. When the eggs are creamy and still slightly runny, whisk in 2 tablespoons of the butter.

4. Transfer to a plate and top with the remaining butter. Season to taste with salt and pepper.

basics

omelets

Making an Omelet

Making an omelet is practically an art form that requires practice, a good frying pan, and a keen sense of knowing exactly when the egg has reached its ideal texture. The French have a term for this perfection: *moelleuse*, which describes an omelet that is perfectly cooked and creamy on the inside. An omelet should never be dry or spongy.

There are various styles of omelets. A classic French omelet is shaped into a small oval roll after being folded three times in the pan. Its creamy center gently spills out when cut. The surface should be smooth and pale, free from any browning or crispness. To achieve this, you begin by making a creamy scrambled egg mixture in the pan, then fold it into an omelet shape. The key is folding it properly, which is easiest with a slightly slanted, high-sided frying pan.

Another style is the French farmer's omelet, folded like a half-moon with a beautifully browned surface and the flavor of nutty, browned butter. Unlike the classic French omelet, this version is stirred more gently in the pan to allow larger curds to form. It uses only eggs—no water, cream, milk, or crème fraîche. Adding liquids can give the mixture unwanted fluffiness and interfere with the final texture.

Finally, the Japanese *tamagoyaki* is a rolled omelet made with eggs, dashi, soy sauce, mirin, and water. Making a *tamagoyaki* requires a skilled cook, a Japanese square egg pan (called a tamago pan), patience, and time. The omelet is made in layers, with each thin layer rolled up before adding the next, forming a delicate multilayered bundle. It is often sliced into noodle soup or placed on top of nigiri sushi.

In both classical French and traditional Japanese kitchens, mastering the omelet is considered an essential skill. In some of the world's best sushi kitchens, it can take years of training to earn the privilege of making the tamagoyaki for guests. Many attempts are rejected by the sushi master, as it requires not only technical skill but also a deep understanding of the craft to become a *shokunin*, the Japanese word for a true master or craftsman.

Tip: Clarified butter is ideal for making a classic French omelet because it contains no milk solids and so doesn't brown easily. To clarify butter, melt butter in a small saucepan over low heat until the milk solids separate and sink to the bottom. Pour the clear, golden fat into a separate bowl, making sure to leave the white milk solids behind. Store clarified butter in a sealed jar in the refrigerator for up to 6 months.

classic french omelet

Makes 1

3 eggs • 1 tablespoon finely chopped herbs, such as chervil, parsley, or chives, plus more for garnish • 1 tablespoon butter (preferably clarified) • flaky salt

1. In a small bowl, whisk the eggs until there are no lumps.
2. Stir in the chopped herbs.
3. Heat a pan over medium heat and add the butter. Let it melt, but not brown. Pour in the egg mixture, quickly shake the pan, and stir with a spatula to create a scrambled-egg-like texture.
4. Tilt the pan so that the mixture flows down and covers the pan. (If you want to add a filling, such as cheese, ham, mushrooms, salmon, or shrimp, do so now but don't overdo it; add just enough so that the omelet can still be easily folded into a nice shape.)
5. Fold the thin part of the omelet over the thicker part.
6. Tap the handle of the pan so the omelet "jumps" over the edge of the pan. (This takes some practice.)
7. Fold the edge over the rest of the omelet and shape it into an oblong round omelet. The surface should be golden yellow, without any browning.
8. Grasp the handle of the pan firmly with a kitchen towel and turn the omelet onto a plate.
9. Sprinkle to taste with herbs and flaky salt before serving. When you cut into the omelet, a creamy egg mixture should spill out.

basics

basics

french farmer's omelet

Makes 1

3 eggs • 2 tablespoons butter, divided • flaky salt • freshly ground black pepper

1. Crack the eggs into a small bowl. Pierce the yolks with a fork (to make them easier to whisk), and whisk the eggs to remove any lumps.
2. Heat a frying pan over medium heat and add 1 tablespoon of the butter.
3. Pour in the egg mixture once the butter has melted and browned. Use a spatula to push the edges of the eggs inward, forming curds. Stop when the eggs begin to set so that the mixture spreads out and forms a round shape. Sprinkle to taste with flaky salt. (If you want to add a filling, such as cheese, ham, mushrooms, salmon, or shrimp, do so now but don't overdo it; add just enough so that the omelet can still be easily folded into a nice shape.)
4. Fold over one half of the omelet while the mixture is still runny.
5. Add the remaining butter to the pan and slide it under the omelet so it gets more color and flavor on the underside.
6. Grasp the handle of the pan firmly with a kitchen towel and turn the omelet onto a plate.
7. Season to taste with pepper and more salt.

tamagoyaki

Makes 1

½ teaspoon salt • 1 ½ teaspoons soy sauce •
¼ teaspoon dashi powder • 1 ½ tablespoons mirin •
1 teaspoon granulated sugar • 5 eggs •
2 tablespoons neutral oil, divided

Special equipment: chopsticks, Japanese omelet pan

1. In a medium bowl, combine ¼ cup (60 ml) water with the salt, soy sauce, dashi, mirin, and sugar. Stir well to dissolve the salt, dashi, and sugar.

2. Crack the eggs into the bowl and whisk with chopsticks until smooth.

3. Heat the Japanese omelet pan over medium heat and add 1 teaspoon of the oil, using a paper towel held with chopsticks to spread the oil evenly over the pan.

4. Pour in a bit of the egg mixture to form a thin layer at the bottom of the pan.

5. Cook over medium heat until the mixture sets—the omelet should not get any color.

6. Roll up the omelet with chopsticks and leave it on one side of the pan.

7. Oil the pan again and pour in more egg mixture, making sure some goes under the rolled omelet so that it "sticks" to the new layer.

8. Starting with the rolled-up layer, roll the omelet again, picking up the second layer. Repeat the process until all the egg is used (ideally at least 5 times). Eventually, you'll have a single thick rolled omelet.

9. Cool the omelet in the refrigerator so it firms up nicely. It can be sliced into soup or noodles or placed on top of nigiri sushi.

63-, 64- & 65-degree eggs

Cooking a 63-Degree Egg

The pursuit of the perfectly cooked egg reached new heights when professional kitchens began using steam ovens and sous vide techniques. These methods, with their precise and consistent temperature control, made it possible to cook eggs to perfection, creating a unique culinary experience. For a while, 63-degree eggs were a highlight on many menus. (Note: The 63, 64, and 65 degrees are all in Celsius, and convert to 145, 147, and 149 degrees Fahrenheit, respectively.)

A 63-degree egg has a delicate, translucent white that just holds together and a soft, runny yolk that remains rich and creamy. Thanks to chefs the world over, this preparation quickly became a sensation, leading to experiments with 64- and 65-degree eggs. Each offers a slightly different texture and flavor. The experience of slicing into a perfectly set, translucent egg with a creamy white and a runny yolk, whether served over a bowl of hot ramen or alongside other dishes, is unlike that of any fried or poached egg.

Why 63 degrees? The egg white and yolk contain various proteins that coagulate at different temperatures. The white begins to set at 61°C (142°F) and fully solidifies at 84°C (183°F), while the yolk starts to thicken between 62°C (149°F) and 65°C (158°F). The so-called "perfect" 63-degree egg represents a middle ground, balancing these points to produce the creamiest soft-cooked egg imaginable.

Instructions:

- Set a sous vide machine or steam oven to 63.5°C (146.3°F)—a slight increase to ensure precision.
- Submerge the eggs in water (if using a sous vide machine) or place them in the steam oven. Cook for 50 minutes.
- Rinse the eggs in cold water to stop the cooking process.
- If you plan to serve them warm, dip the eggs in hot water (about 80°C/176°F) for 2 minutes before serving.
- Gently tap around the middle of the shell with a knife to crack it open. This method prevents breaking the delicate white and allows the yolk to remain intact.

Tip: Fresh eggs yield the best texture, as they have firmer whites. When cooking eggs using sous vide or steam methods, it's normal to see a firmer part of the white alongside a looser part. This happens because the white naturally consists of different layers. Depending on your preference, you can either remove the looser white or leave it as is for a more rustic presentation.

basics

meringue

Whipping Meringue

When egg whites are whipped with sugar and heat is applied, a magical thing happens: they transform into crispy meringues, marshmallows, smooth Italian meringue, French nougat, and soufflés.

You may have heard the old wives' tale that meringue is ready when you can invert the bowl over your head and nothing spills out. This is vague but effective. Meringue must be whipped for a long time to increase volume and ensure the sugar binds well with the egg. If the sugar doesn't dissolve completely, the meringue will bake unevenly and develop small spots of melted sugar on the surface. The goal is to whip the meringue until smooth and glossy, which will yield a crispy exterior with a chewy interior when baked.

Cold-whipped meringue, in which sugar is slowly beaten into already-whipped egg whites, is commonly used for meringue cookies and pavlova and can be used as a pie topping. A more stable option is Swiss meringue, where sugar and egg whites are gently cooked over a water bath to a sticky mixture at 144°F (62°C). When this mixture is whipped until cool, it becomes firm, glossy, and chewy—perfect for oven-baked meringues and Swiss meringue buttercream frosting.

Italian meringue has a different function. Here, hot sugar syrup is whipped into beaten egg whites. As the egg whites and syrup are whipped to a cold meringue, you get a smooth, white, glossy, marshmallow-like cream that can be used for mousse, cake decorations, or as a topping on fruit salad, which can be browned with a blowtorch. (The key distinction between Swiss and Italian meringue lies in the order and temperature at which sugar is incorporated, which affects texture and stability.)

Italian meringue can also be frozen in small bags and used later as a topping for desserts. (Thaw by placing meringues on a wire rack and leaving them out for an hour at room temperature.)

Small amounts of vinegar, lemon juice, or other acid help stabilize meringue and create a smoother texture. Acids cause the proteins to contract, giving the mixture a firmer structure. Additionally, the acid balances the sweetness of the sugar, creating a more pleasant taste.

The amount of sugar varies from recipe to recipe and chef to chef. Traditionally, it's common to weigh the sugar and eggs using a 2:1 sugar-to-egg ratio. This makes a very sweet meringue, with as much sugar as the egg white can bind. However, I've tested and perfected meringue recipes with a bit less sugar than usual, resulting in a fluffier texture and better end product for crispy-chewy meringues and for smooth, glossy Italian meringue.

Tip: When making dishes that call only for egg yolks, remember that the remaining egg whites can be frozen and later thawed and whipped into meringue. Just remember to label the bag with the weight or number of egg whites. Allow them to thaw in the refrigerator before use.

Temperature & Time

Meringues should never be baked above 225°F (110°C). If the heat is higher, they risk developing too much color or cooking too quickly, resulting in a hard shell with a loose interior. Bake on the lower rack of the oven at 225°F (110°C). Small meringues need about 1 hour, while a cake base or large pavlova needs about 1 ½ hours. For extra crispy and dry meringues, let them sit in the oven as they cool, without exposure to outside air or moisture.

basics

classic cold-whipped meringue

Makes about 60 mini meringues or 2 cake bases

3 eggs • 1 teaspoon lemon juice or white vinegar • ¾ cup (180 g) granulated sugar

Special equipment: stand mixer fitted with the whisk attachment or hand mixer

1. Separate the egg whites and yolks and place the whites in a very clean stainless-steel bowl, making sure no traces of yolk remain in the whites. Reserve the yolks for another use.

2. Using the mixer, whip the egg whites with the lemon juice or vinegar until foamy. Gradually add the sugar.

3. Whip the meringue to stiff peaks, checking that all sugar crystals have dissolved (check by rubbing a bit of the mixture between your fingers).

4. The mixture is ready to be piped into small meringues or a cake base and baked.

italian meringue

Makes about 60 mini meringues or 2 cake bases

4 eggs • 1 ⅓ cups plus 3 tablespoons (330 g) granulated sugar, divided

Special equipment: candy thermometer, stand mixer fitted with the whisk attachment or hand mixer

1. Separate the egg whites and yolks and place the whites in a very clean stainless-steel bowl, making sure no traces of yolk remain in the whites. Reserve the yolks for another use.

2. In a saucepan, bring 1 ⅓ cups (300 g) of the sugar and 1 cup (240 ml) water to a boil without stirring.

3. When the temperature reaches about 239°F (115°C), use the mixer to whip the egg whites. Once foamy, add the remaining 3 tablespoons sugar, and whip to soft peaks.

4. Once the sugar mixture reaches 250–253°F (121–123°C), remove it from the heat.

5. Continue to whip the egg whites while pouring the hot syrup into the egg whites in a thin stream. Whip the meringue until all syrup is incorporated and the meringue reaches the desired peaks (soft, medium, or stiff).

6. The meringue is now ready to be used for mousse, cake and pie toppings, and cookies or frozen for later use.

swiss meringue

Makes about 60 mini meringues or 2 cake bases

4 eggs • 1 ¼ cups (270 g) granulated sugar • 2 teaspoons white vinegar

Special equipment: candy thermometer, stand mixer fitted with the whisk attachment or hand mixer

1. Separate the egg whites and yolks and place the whites in a very clean stainless-steel bowl, making sure no traces of yolk remain in the whites. Reserve the yolks for another use.

2. Add the sugar and vinegar to the egg whites and place the bowl over a pot of simmering water (the bowl shouldn't touch the water).

3. Whisk constantly until the mixture reaches 144°F (62°C) and the sugar dissolves. Remove from heat and continue whisking until cool and stiff peaks form.

4. The meringue is now ready to be used for mousse, cake and pie toppings, and cookies or frozen for later use.

emulsions

An emulsified sauce is made by combining a bit of liquid (such as water, vinegar, or wine) with some type of fat (such as butter or oil). Often, but not always, the sauce will also contain egg yolks or whole eggs—examples include mayonnaise, béarnaise, aioli, and hollandaise. These ingredients don't naturally blend together, as the fat would typically separate from the liquid. However, with the right temperature, proper measurements, vigorous whisking, and the gradual addition of fat, you can create a smooth, creamy sauce that's perfect for freshly seared fish, a rare steak, or an egg-and-shrimp sandwich.

My half-French friend Rachel insists that, according to classic French tradition, mayonnaise or aioli should always be stirred with a wooden spoon or made with a mortar and pestle. That's too much effort for me; I prefer to make my mayonnaise quickly. I use a balloon whisk and a bowl with a rounded bottom, which makes it easy to incorporate the oil into the egg mixture. While it might not have the same ritualistic feel as slowly adding oil and watching the mayonnaise thicken as you stir carefully, my method is consistently successful and produces a creamy result. When whisking, I place a damp towel or dishcloth under the bowl to keep it steady on the countertop.

It's best if all ingredients are at room temperature when making mayonnaise or aioli, and lukewarm when making béarnaise or hollandaise. Temperature is the most crucial factor, particularly for béarnaise or hollandaise. The butter shouldn't be too hot when whisked into the egg mixture; if it is, the sauce will break and turn into a thin soup or even scrambled eggs.

With mayonnaise, you can usually achieve a creamy sauce even if the eggs are slightly colder than the oil. However, to ensure the best results, it's a good idea to bring the eggs to room temperature before whisking the mayonnaise together.

Saving a Broken Béarnaise

If your béarnaise breaks, the best trick is to boil a few tablespoons of cream or water in a new pan. Remove it from the heat and slowly whisk the broken sauce into the water to bring it back together. Another option is to whisk 1 tablespoon of ice-cold water into the sauce. This usually helps rebind the sauce, though it may break again later. The same principle applies to mayonnaise: if you've added too much oil and the mixture breaks, start fresh with a new egg in a separate bowl. Gradually whisk in the broken mixture until you have a creamy texture.

Trouble Getting the Mayonnaise Creamy?

If your mayonnaise isn't turning out creamy, your eggs might be too cold, making it difficult for the emulsion process to begin. Another possible reason is not using enough oil. You'll need about ½ to ¾ cup (120–180 ml) of oil per egg yolk. The more oil you add, the thicker the mayonnaise will become. The same principle applies to adding butter to béarnaise or hollandaise. If you want a thinner mayonnaise for use as a dressing, add less oil; for a very thick mayonnaise, where the whisk can almost stand up on its own in the sauce, add more oil. But be cautious—there is a limit to how much oil or butter the mixture can absorb. If you add too much, the sauce will break and won't hold together.

mayonnaise & aioli

Makes about ½ cup (120 ml)

1 egg yolk • 2 teaspoons white wine vinegar • ½ teaspoon Dijon mustard • 1 garlic clove, finely grated (for aioli) • ½ to ¾ cup (120-180 ml) neutral oil, such as canola or sunflower • salt

1. Whisk together the egg yolk, vinegar, and mustard in a bowl. If making aioli, add garlic as well.
2. Gradually whisk in the oil, drop by drop, to form a thick mayonnaise. Season with salt and additional vinegar if necessary.

american-style whole-egg mayonnaise

This American mayonnaise is different from the yolk-heavy European kind. It's made with whole eggs and has a firm, thick consistency—perfect for a club sandwich or a burger. If you've tried Hellmann's mayonnaise, this is similar.

The easiest way to make whole-egg mayonnaise is to use an immersion blender, which instantly creates a creamy result.

Makes about 1 ½ cups (360 ml)

1 egg • 2 teaspoons white wine vinegar • 1 tablespoon Dijon mustard • 1 ½ cups (360 ml) neutral oil, such as canola or sunflower • salt

Special equipment: immersion blender

1. Crack the egg into the immersion blender cup or another tall, narrow container.
2. Add the vinegar and mustard.
3. Pour in the oil.
4. Lower the immersion blender to the bottom of the container and blend until a thick mayonnaise forms. Season with salt and more vinegar if needed.

hollandaise

Hollandaise sauce should be creamy but still thin enough so it slowly coats a poached egg on an eggs Benedict or drizzles over pan-seared fish. I like my hollandaise with a strong citrus flavor, so I finish with lemon juice and adjust the acidity to taste.

Makes about 1 ¼ cups (300 ml)

14 tablespoons butter • 1 shallot, chopped • 2 tablespoons white wine vinegar • ¼ cup (60 ml) dry white wine • 4 whole white peppercorns • 1 parsley sprig • 3 egg yolks • 2 teaspoons lemon juice • salt • freshly ground white pepper

1. Melt the butter in a saucepan. Remove from heat.
2. In a separate pan, combine ¼ cup (60 ml) water with the shallot, vinegar, water, wine, peppercorns, and parsley. Bring to a boil and reduce by half. Remove the shallot, peppercorns, and parsley. Let cool.
3. Whisk the egg yolks into the reduced liquid, then place the pan over low heat and whisk until the mixture thickens.
4. Remove from heat and slowly whisk in the melted butter until creamy. If the sauce gets too thick, add a bit of water.
5. Add the lemon juice and season with salt and pepper to taste.

Tips:

- **Sauce Noisette:** For a slight variation on traditional hollandaise, brown the butter until it has a nutty caramel aroma and turns golden brown. Whisk constantly to prevent the browned proteins from sticking to the bottom (all the flavor is in those little browned bits). Let the butter cool slightly before whisking it into the hollandaise to make this French-style sauce. It's especially delicious with grilled fish or mushrooms.
- **Browned Butter & Soy Hollandaise:** Prepare as for sauce noisette, but whisk 2 tablespoons soy sauce into the vinegar mixture. Try serving this sauce with grilled or broiled fish.

béarnaise

Béarnaise sauce should be slightly firmer and thicker than hollandaise. It should be thick enough to dip fries into or add a generous dollop on top of a steak, so every bite has a creamy touch of sauce on the fork.

For a more umami-rich variation of béarnaise, make sauce choron: sauté 1 ½ tablespoons of tomato paste briefly in a bit of butter until it becomes sweet and concentrated, then whisk it into the sauce along with the egg yolks. Serve with grilled meats.

Makes about 1 ½ cups (360 ml)

20 tablespoons butter • 2 shallots, finely chopped • 3 tablespoons white wine vinegar • 1 parsley sprig • 3 teaspoons finely chopped tarragon, divided • 4 whole white peppercorns • 3 egg yolks • salt

1. Melt the butter in a saucepan and set aside. Gently remove any foam on the surface with a spoon.
2. In a separate saucepan, combine 3 tablespoons water with the shallots, vinegar, parsley, 2 teaspoons of the tarragon, and the peppercorns. Bring to a simmer and reduce liquid by half, then strain and discard the solids. (If desired, keep a bit of the shallots to add back to the sauce at the end for extra flavor, although this is a nontraditional twist.)
3. Pour the vinegar mixture back into the saucepan and let cool. Add the egg yolks and then whisk constantly over low heat until a thick cream forms. (If the mixture feels too hot, remove from heat and keep whisking.)
4. Remove from heat and gradually whisk in the melted butter to form a thick sauce.
5. Season with the remaining tarragon, salt to taste, and any reserved shallots.

Tip: Béarnaise has a short shelf life and should be served à la minute (immediately after being made), while still slightly warm or at room temperature. As long as the accompanying dish is warm, the sauce won't feel too cold. Don't refrigerate béarnaise (the butter will solidify, turning it into a spread) and don't reheat it either. It's a common mistake to try to warm it back up, but the sauce will break and resemble soup.

nobis dressing

This sauce or dressing is lighter than béarnaise and is often served as a salad dressing or with grilled seafood.

Makes about ½ cup (120 ml)

1 egg • 2 teaspoons white wine vinegar • 1 teaspoon Dijon mustard • ½ cup (120 ml) neutral oil, such as canola or sunflower • ½ garlic clove, finely grated • 1 tablespoon finely chopped chives • 1–2 teaspoons lemon juice • salt • freshly ground black pepper

1. Fill a small saucepan half full with water and bring to a simmer. Gently lower the egg into the water and cook for exactly 3 minutes.
2. Cool the egg in cold water, crack the shell, and, using a spoon, scrape the yolk and white into a bowl.
3. Add vinegar and mustard and whisk until the mixture is smooth, with no large lumps.
4. Gradually whisk in the oil to create a thick, creamy sauce.
5. Mix in the garlic and chives. Add the lemon juice and season with salt and pepper to taste.

herb mayonnaise

Makes about 1 ¼ cups (300 ml)

2 egg yolks • 1 garlic clove, peeled • 1 tablespoon finely chopped basil • 1 tablespoon finely chopped dill • 1 tablespoon finely chopped parsley • 1 ½ tablespoons lemon juice • 1 ½ teaspoons grainy mustard • 1 cup (240 ml) neutral oil, such as canola or sunflower • salt • freshly ground black pepper

Special equipment: blender or food processor

1. Using the blender or food processor, blend the egg yolks, garlic, basil, dill, parsley, lemon juice, and mustard. (A blender will create a smooth mayonnaise with a uniform green color, while a food processor may leave small bits of herbs.)
2. Gradually mix in the oil, drop by drop, until you reach a thick mayonnaise consistency. Season with salt, pepper, and more lemon juice to taste.

Tip: For a terrific and easy snack, mix the herb mayonnaise with 3 ½ ounces (100 g) finely grated Parmesan. Spread on toasted baguette slices and bake in the oven at 475°F (250°C) for a couple of minutes. Serve as an appetizer or as an accompaniment to soup or salad.

sauce gribiche

Rather than being a smooth sauce, gribiche draws texture from chopped hard-boiled egg, cornichons, capers, and herbs. Serve it in the spring with steamed asparagus.

Makes about 1 ¼ cups (300 ml)

1 cooked 8-minute egg (page 10) • 1 tablespoon Dijon mustard • 1 teaspoon white wine vinegar • ¼ cup (60 ml) olive oil • 1 tablespoon finely chopped cornichons • 2 tablespoons capers • 1 tablespoon finely chopped parsley • ½ teaspoon finely chopped tarragon • salt • freshly ground black pepper

1. Peel and chop the cooked egg.
2. In a medium bowl, whisk together the mustard and vinegar. Whisk in the oil to create a thick emulsion, then mix in the cornichons, capers, parsley, and tarragon.
3. Stir in the chopped egg and season to taste with salt and pepper.

caesar dressing

Makes about ¾ cup (180 ml)

1 egg yolk • 1 garlic clove, finely grated • 2 teaspoons white wine vinegar • 1 teaspoon Dijon mustard • ¼ cup (60 ml) olive oil • ¼ cup (60 ml) neutral oil, such as canola or sunflower • 3 anchovy fillets, finely chopped • 1 ½ tablespoons capers, coarsely chopped • ¼ cup (30 g) finely grated Parmesan • 1 tablespoon lemon juice • salt • freshly ground black pepper

1. In a medium bowl, whisk together the egg yolk, garlic, vinegar, and mustard.
2. Gradually whisk in the olive oil and neutral oil to form a thick mayonnaise.
3. Mix in the anchovies and capers.
4. Fold in the Parmesan and stir in the lemon juice. Season to taste with salt and pepper and more lemon juice if desired.

soy mayonnaise

This sauce is addictive. Try substituting 1 ½ tablespoons wasabi paste for the soy sauce for a mayo with enough kick to make your eyes water.

Makes about 1 cup (240 ml)

¼ cup (60 ml) soy sauce • 1 egg yolk • 1 tablespoon rice vinegar • 2 teaspoons finely grated ginger • 1 teaspoon sesame oil • ¾ cup (180 ml) neutral oil, such as canola or sunflower • salt

1. In a small saucepan, bring the soy sauce to a boil and reduce to 1 ½ tablespoons. Let cool completely.
2. In a bowl, whisk together the reduced soy sauce, egg yolk, vinegar, and ginger.
3. Gradually whisk in the sesame oil and neutral oil to form a thick mayonnaise.
4. Season to taste with salt.

béarnaise

soy mayonnaise

— *whole-egg mayonnaise*

mayonnaise —

sauce gribiche

Breakfast & Brunch

The egg is a near-perfect food not only because it's a complete source of protein and packed with healthy fats and antioxidants, but because its uses are wildly diverse. Whether you fry it, scramble it, poach it, or whisk it into a batter, an egg for breakfast is the ultimate way to start the day.

breakfast & brunch

full english breakfast

Makes 2 servings

1 (15-ounce/425-g) can small white beans, such as cannellini
½ yellow onion, finely chopped
4 tablespoons butter, divided
2 teaspoons tomato paste
⅛ teaspoon ground allspice
⅛ teaspoon ground coriander
1 (7-ounce/200-g) can crushed tomatoes
1 tablespoon granulated sugar
½ teaspoon Worcestershire sauce
1 tablespoon Brown Sauce HP-Style (page 78)
1 teaspoon white wine vinegar
Salt
10 ½ ounces (300 g) fresh breakfast sausage links
5 ounces (140 g) bacon
2 small portobello mushrooms
5 ½ ounces (150 g) cherry tomatoes on the vine
4 small eggs
Toast, for serving

Special equipment: immersion blender

1. Rinse and drain the beans.
2. In a large saucepan, sauté the onion in 1 tablespoon of the butter. Add tomato paste, allspice, and coriander, and sauté for a few minutes.
3. Add ½ cup (120 ml) water, and the crushed tomatoes, sugar, Worcestershire sauce, HP sauce, and vinegar. Simmer for about 15 minutes.
4. Using the immersion blender, blend the sauce until smooth. Add the beans and let them simmer for an additional 10 minutes. Season with salt.
5. In a separate pan, fry the sausages in 1 tablespoon of the butter until they have nice color. Add ¼ cup (60 ml) of water to the pan, cover with a lid, and let the sausages steam until fully cooked through.
6. Set the sausages aside, and fry the bacon in the same pan until crispy. Set aside with the sausages.
7. Using the same pan, fry the mushrooms and tomatoes in 1 tablespoon of the butter. Season to taste with salt. Set aside and rinse the pan.
8. In the same pan, melt the remaining 1 tablespoon butter. Crack 2 eggs at a time into a small bowl.
9. Slide the eggs into the warm pan, frying them together like one egg with two yolks. Season to taste with salt.
10. Reheat the sausage, bacon, tomatoes, and mushrooms in the pan.
11. Serve the eggs and other ingredients with beans and toast.

Tip: HP sauce, named after the UK's House of Parliament, is the British equivalent of steak sauce.

A full English breakfast isn't something you eat daily, but it is the ultimate breakfast. It will keep you satisfied throughout the day with the perfect combination of eggs, sausage, and bacon. It's also one of the best "pick-me-ups" after a late night.

You can vary the eggs, whether scrambled, poached, or fried. In England, you can also choose the type of bacon—American-style with more fat, or British butcher-style, which resembles thinly sliced pork chops. So many choices, but always a complete breakfast.

full english breakfast

breakfast & brunch

egg muffin

Perhaps one of the few things to thank McDonald's for is the Egg McMuffin, the buttery, toasted English muffin topped with Canadian bacon or sausage, a fried egg, and cheese. It's truly a perfect breakfast sandwich.

While you can use store-bought English muffins, this accompanying recipe is easy since the dough is cold-proofed and then fried in a pan instead of baked in the oven. These muffins are quick to make, and any leftovers can be frozen—just slice them in half first so the frozen halves can go straight into the toaster.

Makes 16

1 ⅔ cups (400 ml) warm water
2 ¼ teaspoons dry active yeast
4 ¼ cups (510 g) all-purpose flour, plus more for dusting
½ teaspoon salt
⅔ cup (120 g) cornmeal
Neutral oil or butter, for frying

English Muffins

1. Place the warm water in a large bowl. Stir in yeast and allow to bloom for 5 minutes.
2. Add the flour and knead into a smooth dough. Add the salt towards the end of kneading and incorporate it into the dough.
3. Cover the bowl with plastic wrap and let rise at room temperature at least 6 hours or overnight.
4. Pour the cornmeal onto a plate or shallow dish.
5. Turn the dough out onto a floured surface and divide it into 16 equal pieces. Shape each piece into a round ball and press into the cornmeal. Turn them over so the cornmeal covers both the top and bottom. Flatten slightly.
6. When ready to eat, fry each muffin in a bit of oil or butter over low heat for about 8 minutes on each side.
7. Let cool and cut in half. Toast before serving.

Makes 2 servings

2 English Muffins (see above)
2 tablespoons butter, divided
4 slices cheese, such as Gouda, Edam, or cheddar
2 eggs
5 ½ ounces (150 g) Canadian bacon, sliced
Homemade Ketchup and Brown Sauce HP-Style (pages 78 and 79), for serving (optional)

Egg Muffins

1. Preheat the oven to 300°F (150°C).
2. Slice the English muffins in half and, in a frying pan, toast them on both sides in 1 tablespoon of the butter.
3. Remove 2 halves and place cut side up on a baking sheet. Place 2 cheese slices on each of the halves. Bake for about 5 minutes, until the cheese melts.
4. While the halves are in the oven, fry the eggs in the remaining butter, leaving the yolk runny or creamy, based on your preference.
5. Remove the muffin halves from the oven and top with Canadian bacon and the fried eggs. Place the other muffin half on top. Serve with ketchup and HP sauce.

huevos rancheros

There are numerous variations of this Mexican breakfast favorite. Sometimes it's served in a pan with eggs poached in a chili-tomato sauce, and other times, it's served in deep bowls topped with eggs, or presented on a platter. The onion can be fried or pickled (or both), and the cheese might be queso fresco or grated American cheddar. The truth is, there's no right or wrong way to make this farmer's breakfast, which evolved in much the same way as hash—leftovers from dinner were eaten for breakfast the next day. This version uses fried tortillas for a crunchy contrast to the soft beans, sauce, and eggs. If you're extra hungry, add rice with the beans.

Makes 2 servings

Huevos Rancheros

1 red onion, thinly sliced
1 teaspoon granulated sugar
1 ½ teaspoons white wine vinegar
⅛ teaspoon salt
⅔ cup (160 ml) neutral oil, such as canola or sunflower, plus more for frying eggs
4 small corn tortillas
½ can (7 ½ ounces/213 g) black beans, drained and rinsed
1 avocado, diced
2 eggs
4 tablespoons Mexican crema
½ bunch cilantro, chopped
1 ¾ ounces (50 g) grated or crumbled Cotija cheese
Salt and freshly ground black pepper
½ lime, cut into wedges

Sauce

1 teaspoon cumin seeds
1 teaspoon coriander seeds
2 tablespoons olive oil
1 teaspoon smoked paprika
½ yellow onion, finely chopped
½ garlic clove, finely chopped
½ red chili pepper, such as red jalapeño or Fresno, seeded and finely chopped
1 (15-ounce/425-g) can crushed tomatoes
salt and freshly ground black pepper

Special equipment: deep-fry thermometer

1. In a bowl, mix the red onion, sugar, vinegar, and ⅛ teaspoon salt. Let sit at room temperature for at least 30 minutes, tossing occasionally.

2. Make the sauce: in a spice grinder, grind the cumin and coriander. In a large skillet or saucepan with a lid over medium heat, warm the oil and add the cumin, coriander, and paprika. Add the onion, garlic, and chili, and sauté for a few minutes until the onion softens. Add the crushed tomatoes and 3 tablespoons water. Bring to a simmer, then cover the pan and let simmer for 15 minutes. Remove the lid and simmer for 5 more minutes. Season with salt and pepper to taste.

3. In a frying pan over medium heat, warm the neutral oil to 350°F (175°C). Lower the tortillas into the oil carefully, and fry one at a time until they are golden and crispy. Let drain on paper towels.

4. In a medium bowl, combine the black beans and diced avocado.

5. Fry the eggs in oil until crispy.

6. Place the tortillas slightly overlapping on a plate. Top one tortilla with the black bean and avocado mixture and a dollop of crema. Top the other tortilla with warm tomato sauce and an egg. Sprinkle with cilantro, Cotija, and salt and pepper. Repeat for the remaining ingredients.

7. Serve with lime wedges.

breakfast burrito

It's hard to find a diner in America that doesn't have a breakfast burrito on the menu: flour tortillas filled with eggs, cheese, peppers, sausage or bacon, and sometimes rice, beans, and tomato. For this dish, scrambled eggs are best because they'll hold up to the other fillings.

Makes 2 burritos

1 tablespoon olive oil

1 yellow onion, sliced

1 red bell pepper, seeded and sliced

2 fresh chorizo sausages, halved

2 servings Scrambled Eggs in a Frying Pan (page 22)

½ jalapeño, seeded and finely chopped

⅔ cup (65 g) grated cheddar cheese

Salt

2 large flour tortillas

1 tomato, diced

½ bunch cilantro, roughly chopped

1. In a skillet over medium heat, warm the oil and sauté the onion and bell pepper for about 5 minutes. Set aside on a plate.

2. In the same skillet, fry the chorizo for about 10 minutes, until fully cooked. Remove chorizo to a cutting board and coarsely chop. Wash the frying pan.

3. Prepare the scrambled eggs, adding the jalapeño towards the end of cooking. Top with the cheese and add salt to taste.

4. Warm the tortillas and top each one with half the eggs, sausage, vegetables, tomato, and cilantro. Roll up the burritos, folding in the sides so the filling stays put. Wrap in parchment paper or aluminum foil if desired, cut in half, and serve.

breakfast & brunch

croque madame

The difference between a croque madame and a croque monsieur—two of France's most iconic sandwiches—is the egg. Whereas a golden fried egg crowns the croque madame like a hat, the croque monsieur is hatless. In either case, the sandwiches are composed of stacks of bread, ham, cheese, and creamy béchamel sauce.

Makes 2 sandwiches

Béchamel

1 tablespoon butter

1 tablespoon all-purpose flour

⅔ cup (160 ml) whole milk

1 ¾ ounces (50 g) finely grated Comté or Gruyère cheese

1 ½ teaspoons whole-grain Dijon mustard

1 ½ teaspoons finely grated horseradish

⅛ teaspoon grated nutmeg

Salt and freshly ground black pepper

Sandwiches

2 tablespoons butter, divided

4 slices white bread, preferably sourdough

2 tablespoons whole-grain Dijon mustard

8 slices cooked ham

4 slices (about 4 ounces/120 g) Comté or Gruyère cheese

2 eggs

Salt and freshly ground black pepper

1 tablespoon finely chopped chives

1. Preheat the oven to 425°F (225°C).

2. Make the béchamel: in a saucepan, melt the butter and whisk in the flour. Cook briefly, then whisk in the milk until smooth. Let simmer into a thick sauce for about 3 minutes. Remove from heat and whisk in the cheese, mustard, horseradish, and nutmeg. Season with salt and pepper to taste.

3. Make the sandwiches: In a frying pan over medium heat, melt 1 tablespoon of the butter and toast the bread slices on each side until golden brown.

4. Spread mustard on the toasted bread. Line a baking sheet with parchment paper and top with 2 slices of bread. To each slice of bread, add 4 slices of ham and 1 slice of cheese.

5. Place the remaining slices of bread on top. Pour over a generous amount of béchamel and top with the remaining cheese slices.

6. Place the baking sheet in the center of the oven and cook for about 5 minutes, until the cheese is melted and bubbly.

7. While the sandwiches are cooking, melt the remaining 1 tablespoon butter in a frying pan and fry the eggs sunny-side up (Classic French Fried Egg, page 14), keeping the yolks runny. Season with salt and pepper.

8. Remove the sandwiches from the oven and top each one with an egg.

9. Garnish with chives and serve immediately.

croque madame

egg sandwich

This creamy scramble served on brioche with caramelized onions, cheese, and bacon is an instant classic. When the food truck Eggslut began roaming the streets of Los Angeles in 2011, the gourmet egg sammy shot onto the food scene like a comet. Within a few years, many other places followed suit, adding dressed-up sandwiches to their breakfast and brunch menus.

Makes 2 sandwiches

2 tablespoons butter, divided
1 yellow onion, sliced
Salt
5 ounces (140 g) bacon
1 recipe scrambled eggs (Scrambled Eggs in a Frying Pan, page 22)
3 tablespoons finely chopped chives
Freshly ground black pepper
2 Brioche Buns (page 61)
2–4 slices cheddar, Gouda, or American cheese

1. Preheat the oven to 300°F (150°C).
2. In a large skillet over medium heat, melt 1 tablespoon of the butter and add the onions and ⅓ teaspoon salt. Sauté for about 10 minutes, until soft and caramelized. Remove to a plate.
3. In the same skillet, fry the bacon over medium heat until crispy. Transfer to paper towels. Wipe out the skillet.
4. Prepare the scrambled eggs, stir in the chives, and season to taste with salt and pepper.
5. Line a baking sheet with parchment paper. In the skillet over medium heat, melt the remaining 1 tablespoon of butter. Halve the brioche buns and place in the skillet, cut side down. Toast until golden. Place the bottoms of the buns on the baking sheet and top each with 1–2 slices of cheese. Transfer to the oven until the cheese is melted.
6. Top the brioche bun bottoms with scrambled eggs, bacon, caramelized onions, and bun tops. Serve immediately.

boiled eggs & soldiers

The art of a perfectly boiled egg shines through in this simple breakfast. The eggs should have creamy, runny yolks in which to dip the crispy lengths of toast.

Makes 2 servings

5 ½ tablespoons butter, divided

3 shallots, 1 finely chopped and 2 sliced

Salt

½ anchovy fillet, finely chopped

1 tablespoon finely chopped thyme

1 tablespoon finely chopped chives

1 teaspoon white wine vinegar

2 teaspoons olive oil

2 eggs

4 slices white sandwich bread

1 bunch watercress or baby arugula

1. In a skillet over medium heat, melt 1 tablespoon of the butter and add the chopped shallot (reserving the two sliced shallots) a pinch of salt. Sauté for 2 minutes.

2. In a small bowl, mash the sautéed shallot with 3 ½ tablespoons of the butter and the anchovy, thyme, and chives. Refrigerate, and remove about 20 minutes before serving to soften.

3. In a medium bowl, combine the sliced shallots, vinegar, olive oil, and a pinch of salt. Let stand for about 10 minutes.

4. Simmer 2 eggs for 5 minutes (pages 9-10 for instructions).

5. Cut the bread into thin sticks. In the skillet over medium heat, melt the remaining 1 tablespoon of butter in a skillet. Add the bread and fry, turning until golden. Let cool slightly.

6. Toss the watercress in the shallot/vinegar mixture. Cut the tops off the eggs and place in egg cups. Serve with the watercress salad, herb butter, and crispy toast soldiers.

eggs florentine

breakfast & brunch

brioche

Makes 2 loaves

1 ½ cups (360 ml) whole milk, warmed to 100°F–115°F (38°C–46°C)

¼ cup (50 g) granulated sugar

2 ½ teaspoons active dry yeast

2 eggs

4 cups (480 g) all-purpose flour, divided

1 teaspoon baking powder

2 teaspoons salt

⅔ cup (150 g) butter, at room temperature

1 egg, beaten, for brushing

Special equipment: candy thermometer, stand mixer fitted with a dough hook (optional)

1. In a large bowl, combine the warmed milk and the sugar. Sprinkle the yeast on top, then gently stir into the milk. Allow the yeast to bloom for 5 minutes.
2. Add the eggs and stir well.
3. Pour the bloomed yeast, milk, and egg mixture into the bowl of the stand mixer or into a large bowl.
4. In a small bowl, combine ½ cup (60 g) of the flour with the baking powder. Add this mixture to the bowl with the yeast, milk, and eggs, and mix on low speed (or by hand) until incorporated. Add the rest of the flour gradually, mixing until incorporated.
5. Add salt and butter and knead until dough is smooth and doesn't stick to itself or the bowl. If necessary, add more flour. Cover with plastic wrap and let rise at room temperature for about 2 hours.
6. Divide dough into 2 equal pieces and transfer into greased loaf pans.
7. Cover with a kitchen towel or loosely draped plastic wrap, allowing space for the dough to rise without sticking. Let it rise for 1 hour at room temperature.
8. Preheat the oven to 440°F (225°C) and brush loaves with the beaten egg.
9. Bake in the center of the oven for about 40 minutes. Let the loaves cool in their pans before removing.

Tip: To make brioche buns for dishes like the Egg Sandwich (page 56), use the same recipe and, instead of dividing the dough into 2 loaf pans, line 2 baking sheets with parchment. Divide the dough into 20 pieces and roll the pieces into round buns. Place on the baking sheets, flatten slightly with your palm, and cover and let rise for about 2 ½ hours. When ready to bake, preheat the oven to 400°F (200°C). Brush the buns with the beaten egg and bake for about 15 minutes until deeply golden.

eggs benedict

There are a few variations on the story behind eggs Benedict, the quintessential brunch dish. One popular version traces its roots to the late 1800s, when a recipe called "eggs à la Benedick" appeared in a cookbook by Charles Ranhofer, the chef at Delmonico's in New York City. This recipe featured two poached eggs topped with creamy hollandaise, and is similar to what we know today.

Another (perhaps more entertaining) story involves Lemuel Benedict, a New York financier. In the 1940s, after a long night of partying, he arrived at the Waldorf Hotel for breakfast and ordered toasted and buttered bread topped with two poached eggs, bacon, and hollandaise. The hotel chefs were impressed by the combination, made a few modifications, and eventually added it to their menu—replacing the bacon with ham and serving it on a toasted English muffin. Thus, the modern version of eggs Benedict was born: a toasted English muffin topped with Canadian bacon, poached eggs, and creamy hollandaise.

For an extra touch of indulgence, this recipe uses a brioche-style bread, adding a buttery flavor and creating a deliciously crispy base for the eggs.

Makes 2 servings

1 tablespoon butter
2 slices brioche (page 61)
3 ½ ounces (100 g) sliced Canadian bacon
4 poached eggs (page 17)
1 recipe hollandaise (page 39)
1 ½ teaspoons finely chopped chives
Flaky sea salt

1. In a large skillet over medium heat, melt the butter and then add the brioche. Toast on both sides until golden and crispy.
2. Remove the brioche to 2 plates and top each one with Canadian bacon, 2 poached eggs, and hollandaise.
3. Sprinkle with chives and flaky salt.

Tip: For a healthier take on eggs Benedict, replace the Canadian bacon with 7 ounces (200 g) of sautéed spinach for Eggs Florentine.

eggs benedict with mushroom & fennel hollandaise

Makes 2 servings

½ teaspoon ground fennel

1 recipe hollandaise (page 39)

2 tablespoons butter, divided

2 slices brioche (page 61)

14 ounces (400 g) oyster mushrooms, torn into bite-size pieces

Zest of ½ lemon

Flaky sea salt

4 poached eggs (page 17)

1. Stir the fennel into the hollandaise.
2. In a large skillet over medium heat, melt 1 tablespoon of the butter and then add the brioche. Toast on both sides until golden and crispy. Remove the brioche to 2 plates.
3. Melt the remaining 1 tablespoon of butter in the skillet, and sauté the mushrooms until crispy and browned. Season with lemon zest and salt to taste.
4. Top each piece of brioche with mushrooms, 2 poached eggs, and hollandaise.

eggs benedict with salmon & dill-horseradish hollandaise

Makes 2 servings

1 tablespoon lemon juice

1 tablespoon finely chopped dill, plus more for garnish

1 teaspoon finely grated horseradish, plus more for serving

1 recipe hollandaise (page 39)

3 tablespoons butter, divided

2 slices brioche (page 61)

9 ounces (250 g) thin asparagus, woody ends removed, sliced lengthwise

Flaky sea salt

4 slices cold-smoked salmon

4 poached eggs (page 17)

1. Stir the lemon juice, dill, and horseradish into the hollandaise.
2. In a large skillet over medium heat, melt 1 tablespoon of the butter and then add the brioche. Toast on both sides until golden and crispy. Remove the brioche to 2 plates.
3. Melt the remaining 2 tablespoons of butter in the skillet, and sauté the asparagus until tender. Season to taste with salt.
4. Top each piece of brioche with asparagus, 2 slices salmon, 2 poached eggs, and hollandaise. Garnish with flaky salt and extra dill, and serve with additional grated horseradish if desired.

breakfast & brunch

shakshuka

This traditional Tunisian dish features notes of saffron, spicy harissa, cumin, and coriander. The eggs are poached in a rich tomato sauce full of caramelized onions, bitter green peppers, and sweet red peppers.

Makes 4 servings

1 teaspoon whole cumin seeds
1 teaspoon whole coriander seeds
3 tablespoons olive oil
2 yellow onions, finely chopped
½ garlic clove, finely chopped
1 red bell pepper, seeded and chopped
1 green bell pepper, seeded and chopped
1 teaspoon harissa
1 teaspoon paprika
Saffron threads
Turmeric
2 (15-ounce/425-g) cans crushed tomatoes
Salt and freshly ground black pepper
4 eggs
1 bunch cilantro, chopped
1 bunch mint, chopped
Pita or sourdough toast, for serving

Special equipment: mortar and pestle or spice grinder

1. Coarsely grind the cumin and coriander seeds with the mortar and pestle or spice grinder.

2. In a large skillet over medium heat, warm the olive oil and sauté the onions for about 10 minutes until they are sweet, caramelized, and golden brown; this is key to the flavor of the dish.

3. Add the garlic, red and green peppers, harissa, paprika, and a pinch each of saffron threads and turmeric. Cook for about 5 minutes until the vegetables begin to soften.

4. Add the crushed tomatoes and ¾ cup (180 ml) water. Season to taste with salt and pepper.

5. Bring to a simmer, cover the skillet, and let simmer gently for about 15 minutes. Taste and adjust the seasoning, if desired.

6. Using a spoon, create wells in the sauce and crack the eggs into them. Cover the skillet again, and cook for about 8–10 minutes, or until the eggs are done to your preference.

7. Stir in the chopped herbs and serve with pita or toasted sourdough bread.

breakfast & brunch

toasts

There are countless ways an egg can feature in a sandwich: classically hard-boiled and sliced, soft-boiled to run over the bread, fried, poached, chopped… For me, the toasted sourdough slice with mashed avocado, egg, and dukkah from a café in Bushwick in Brooklyn and the classic buttered toast with bacon and fried egg from Towpath Café in East London are among my favorites.

egg & avocado toast

Makes 1 piece of toast

1 tablespoon olive oil
1 slice white sourdough bread
½ avocado
½ lemon
1 boiled 6-minute egg (pages 9–10), peeled
1 teaspoon sesame seeds, toasted and crushed
Flaky sea salt

1. In a skillet over medium heat, warm the oil and then toast the bread on both sides until well browned. Set aside to let cool slightly.
2. In a small bowl, mash the avocado with a squeeze of lemon juice.
3. Top the toast with the avocado mash and the egg. Cut a slit in the egg to let the yolk run over the toast. Sprinkle with sesame seeds and season to taste with salt.

egg & tomato levain toast

Makes 1 piece of toast

2 tablespoons olive oil, divided
1 slice white sourdough levain
4 slices tomato
1 boiled 7-minute egg (pages 9–10), peeled and sliced
Fresh basil leaves
Flaky sea salt
Freshly ground black pepper

1. In a skillet over medium heat, warm 1 tablespoon of the oil and then toast the bread on both sides until well browned. Set aside to let cool slightly.
2. Layer the toast with tomato slices, egg slices, and basil.
3. Drizzle with the remaining 1 tablespoon olive oil and season to taste with salt and pepper.

egg in a basket

Makes 1 piece of toast

1 slice white sandwich bread
2 tablespoons butter
1 egg
Flaky sea salt
Brown Sauce HP-Style (page 78) and Homemade Ketchup (page 79), for serving (optional)

1. Cut a hole in the middle of the bread using the rim of a glass or a cookie cutter.
2. In a skillet over medium heat, melt the butter until it bubbles. Fry the bread gently until golden brown on both sides and fragrant.
3. Crack the egg into the hole and reduce heat to low. Cook until the white is set and the yolk remains runny and creamy.
4. Season to taste with salt and, if desired, serve with HP sauce and ketchup.

soft rye toast with egg & swedish sausage

Makes 1 piece of toast

1 slice classic soft rye bread
2 tablespoons butter, divided
6-8 slices Swedish sausage or other cooked breakfast sausage
1 egg
Flaky sea salt
Freshly ground black pepper
Homemade Ketchup and Homemade Mustard (page 79), for serving

1. Toast the bread in a toaster, then spread one side with 1 tablespoon of the butter.
2. In a skillet over medium heat, melt the remaining 1 tablespoon butter and fry the sliced sausage. Remove from the skillet.
3. To the skillet, add the egg and fry on one side, allowing the white to get a little color and crisp around the edges. Season to taste with salt and pepper.
4. Top the buttered toast with the sausage slices and then the fried egg.
5. Drizzle with ketchup and mustard.

crispbread with egg, potato & sandwich caviar

Makes 1 piece of toast

1 tablespoon butter
1 piece crispbread
2 cold boiled potatoes, sliced
1 boiled 7-minute egg (pages 9–10), peeled and sliced
1 tablespoon sandwich caviar (Swedish smoked cod roe spread, commonly sold in tubes)
Dill fronds, for garnish

1. Spread the butter on the crispbread.
2. Layer the potatoes and egg slices on the crispbread.
3. Top with caviar and garnish with dill.

open-faced rye sandwich with egg & anchovies

Makes 1 piece of toast

1 tablespoon butter
1 slice rye bread
1 boiled 7-minute egg (pages 9–10), peeled and quartered
4 anchovy fillets
1 ½ teaspoons finely sliced chives

1. Spread the butter on the rye bread.
2. Layer the quartered egg and anchovies on the bread. Top with chives.

egg & tunacado toast

Makes 1 piece of toast

1 tablespoon olive oil

1 slice white sourdough bread

¼ cup canned tuna, drained

2 tablespoons American-Style Whole-Egg Mayonnaise (page 39)

2 teaspoons harissa or gochujang (Korean chili paste)

Flaky sea salt

½ avocado, thinly sliced

1 boiled 6-minute egg (pages 9–10), peeled and halved

Korean chili flakes or red pepper flakes

1. In a skillet over medium heat, warm the oil and then toast the bread on both sides until well browned. Set aside to let cool slightly.
2. In a medium bowl, mix the tuna, mayonnaise, and harissa until fairly smooth. Season to taste with salt.
3. Layer the avocado on the toast, followed by the tuna spread and egg halves.
4. Sprinkle to taste with chili flakes and more flaky salt.

Tip: Korean chili flakes (also called gochugaru) are generally milder than red pepper flakes.

egg & mayo toast

Makes 1 piece of toast

2 boiled 9-minute eggs (pages 9–10), peeled and coarsely chopped

2 tablespoons American-Style Whole-Egg Mayonnaise (page 39)

½ teaspoon Dijon mustard

1 slice Danish rye bread, toasted

1 tablespoon finely chopped chives

Flaky sea salt

1. In a medium bowl, mix the chopped eggs, mayonnaise, and Dijon mustard.
2. Top the rye bread with the egg mixture, sprinkle with chives, and season to taste with flaky salt.

This combination of eggs, tomatoes, and chili oil is an umami bomb like no other and makes the perfect breakfast for a lazy weekend morning.

egg & tomato with crunchy chili oil

Makes 4 servings

8 eggs

3 tablespoons neutral oil, divided

4 tomatoes, quartered

4 scallions, white and green parts, divided and sliced

½ teaspoon salt

Cooked rice and Crunchy Chili Oil (below), for serving

1. Beat the eggs. In a large skillet or wok over medium heat, warm 1 tablespoon of the oil. Add the eggs and cook, stirring, to make a rough scramble. When eggs are cooked, remove to a plate.

2. Wipe out the skillet and add the remaining 2 tablespoons of oil. Add the tomatoes and white parts of the scallions. Over medium-high heat, stir-fry until the tomatoes soften. Stir in 3 tablespoons water and the salt.

3. Stir in the scrambled eggs and serve immediately with cooked rice and crunchy chili oil. Garnish with the green parts of the scallions.

crunchy chili oil

Makes about 2 cups (480 ml)

1 ⅔ cups (400 ml) neutral oil

1 yellow onion, finely chopped

8 garlic cloves, finely chopped

4 scallions, green and white parts, finely chopped

1 ½ tablespoons coarsely chopped ginger

3 star anise pods

1 cinnamon stick

3 bay leaves

¼ cup (20 g) red pepper flakes

⅔ cup (60 g) gochugaru (Korean chili flakes)

2 tablespoons fried onion

1 tablespoon sesame oil

3 tablespoons soy sauce

2 teaspoons salt

1. In a medium saucepan over low heat, warm the oil and add the onion, garlic, scallions, ginger, star anise, cinnamon, and bay leaves.

2. Bring to a simmer and let cook for about 15 minutes, until the oil is infused and the onion is lightly browned. Remove from heat.

3. In a large metal bowl, combine the red pepper flakes, gochugaru, fried onion, sesame oil, soy sauce, and salt.

4. Carefully pour the hot oil over the chili mixture. It will sizzle, which is normal, as it indicates that the oil is hot enough to bring out the flavors in the chilies.

5. Stir to combine, then set aside to cool. Once cool, remove the bay leaves, star anise, and cinnamon stick. Transfer the crunchy chili oil to a large lidded jar and store in the refrigerator for up to 3 months.

breakfast & brunch

jianbing

Jianbing is a popular Chinese street food similar to crêpes, in which a thin pancake and egg are cooked together and eaten as a wrap. Professionals spread the batter with a special wooden tool over a hot crêpe iron, making the process look simple, but creating *jianbing* at home takes practice. A crêpe pan or a low-sided skillet works well, and a heat-resistant silicone spatula is perfect for spreading the batter.

Makes 4 servings (8 *jianbing*)

Batter

¾ cup (90 g) all-purpose flour
½ cup (80 g) rice flour
¾ cup (80 g) chickpea flour
1 ½ tablespoons cornstarch
2 ¼ cups (540 ml) cold water
⅕ cup (50 ml) neutral oil
½ teaspoon salt

Fillings and Toppings

3 tablespoons neutral oil
14 ounces (400 g) firm tofu
1 garlic clove, finely chopped
2 teaspoons finely chopped ginger
2 tablespoons soy sauce
4–8 eggs
Hoisin
2 scallions, green parts only, finely sliced
2 tablespoons sesame seeds, toasted
½ cucumber, julienned
1 cup (16 g) chopped cilantro

Special equipment: crêpe pan or low-sided skillet

1. Make the batter: In a large bowl, whisk together the all-purpose flour, rice flour, chickpea flour, and cornstarch. Add the water, oil, and salt, and whisk until smooth. The batter should be slightly thicker than regular pancake batter. Let rest for 10 minutes.

2. While batter rests, make the filling: In a large skillet over medium-high heat, warm the oil. Crumble the tofu into the pan and fry until crispy.

3. Add garlic, ginger, and soy sauce, frying quickly to coat the tofu before the mixture burns. Remove from heat.

4. In a crêpe pan or low-sided skillet over medium heat, pour in a ladleful of the batter (approximately a quarter) and quickly spread it thinly with a spatula to cover the surface of the pan.

5. Once the batter sets, crack 1 or 2 eggs, depending on preference, over the crêpe, break the yolk(s), and spread the egg over the surface.

6. When the egg is set, brush the crêpe with hoisin sauce. Place a scoop of tofu filling in the center and top with a quarter of the scallions, toasted sesame seeds, julienned cucumber, and chopped cilantro. Repeat process for remaining crêpes. Serve open-faced as shown, or fold loosely in half if desired.

brown sauce hp-style

After living in England and enjoying dishes like Cumberland sausage and eggs, full English breakfasts, and bacon sandwiches, I always keep a large bottle of tangy, spice-filled brown sauce in my refrigerator. HP, which is akin to American steak sauce, is a classic English condiment, but there are many copies and variations. The key when making your own is to achieve a peppery kick and a balance of sweetness and acidity.

Makes about 2 ½ cups (600 ml)

½ cup (120 ml) tomato paste

½ cup (120 ml) apple juice, diluted with ½ cup (120 ml) water

1 ¼ cups (300 ml) apple cider vinegar

½ cup (85 g) pitted prunes

5 dried dates, pitted

⅓ cup (35 g) chopped dried tamarind (available in international grocery stores)

¾ cup (150 g) dark muscovado sugar

1 yellow onion, quartered

1 garlic clove, peeled

1 tablespoon finely grated ginger

2 ½ teaspoons black peppercorns

6 cloves

2 whole nutmeg

6 allspice berries

5 cardamom pods

1 teaspoon dry mustard powder, such as Colman's

Mustard seeds

2 teaspoons salt

2 tablespoons distilled white vinegar

3 tablespoons Worcestershire sauce

2 tablespoons fish sauce

Special equipment: immersion blender

1. In a large lidded saucepan, combine the tomato paste, apple juice, vinegar, prunes, dates, tamarind, sugar, onion, garlic, ginger, peppercorns, cloves, nutmeg, allspice, cardamom, dry mustard, a pinch of mustard seeds, salt, vinegar, Worcestershire, and fish sauce. Bring to a boil, then reduce the heat to a simmer and let cook, covered, for 10 minutes.

2. Let cool slightly, then carefully blend the mixture with an immersion blender until smooth. Bring mixture back to a simmer, and cook, covered, for 30 minutes.

3. Pour into sterilized jars, seal in a water bath, and let cool. Store in a cool, dry place for up to 3 months, and refrigerate once opened.

Tip: If you don't want to sterilize jars, you can store the sauce in a tightly sealed container in the refrigerator for up to 2 months.

homemade ketchup

Makes about 1 ⅔ cups (400 ml)

⅔ cup (160 ml) tomato paste
½ cup (120 ml) apple cider vinegar
½ cup (100 g) light muscovado sugar (or brown sugar)
½ yellow onion, quartered
1 clove
2 allspice berries
1 tablespoon Worcestershire sauce
1 teaspoon salt

Special equipment: immersion blender

1. In a large lidded saucepan, combine 1 cup (240 ml) water with the tomato paste, vinegar, sugar, onion, clove, allspice, Worcestershire, and salt, and bring to a boil, covered. Reduce heat to a simmer and cook for 10 minutes.
2. Let cool slightly, then carefully blend the mixture with an immersion blender until smooth. Bring mixture back to a simmer, and cook, covered, for 30 minutes.
3. Pour into sterilized jars, seal in a water bath, and let cool. Store in a cool, dry place for up to 3 months, and refrigerate once opened.

Tips: If you don't want to sterilize jars, you can store the sauce in a tightly sealed container in the refrigerator for up to 2 months. The choice of tomato paste plays a crucial role in the final flavor. For best results, choose an Italian brand with a concentrated tomato flavor. For a chili sauce variation, add 1 seeded, finely chopped red jalapeño and ½ garlic clove to the mixture, and cook with the other ingredients.

homemade mustard

Makes about ¾ cup (180 ml)

½ cup (57 g) dry mustard powder, such as Colman's
1 tablespoon yellow mustard seeds
1 tablespoon brown mustard seeds
2 tablespoons cornstarch
2 tablespoons white wine vinegar
1 tablespoon granulated sugar
2 tablespoons canola oil
1 teaspoon salt

1. In a saucepan, combine the dry mustard, mustard seeds, and cornstarch with ½ cup (120 ml) water. Whisk until smooth.
2. Add the vinegar, sugar, oil, and salt. Pour into a jar and let cool.
3. Seal the jar and let the mustard sit in the refrigerator for at least 3 days to develop a good flavor and consistency. It can be stored in the refrigerator for up to 6 months.

Small dishes & snacks

Although eggs are deservingly the stars of the show at breakfast and brunch, they can make equally good impressions as savory appetizers and snacks.

classic scotch egg

In this classic British pub snack, a soft-boiled egg is wrapped in sausage and fried. The result is a savory outer crust and a creamy filling—a combo that seems almost tailor-made for a pint of ale. Wrapping soft-boiled eggs in sausage meat can be tricky, but with practice (and plastic wrap), you'll achieve full coverage. When the eggs are fried, the sausage expands a little, and sometimes cracks can appear in the coating. To avoid this, maintain a consistent oil temperature so the oil doesn't get too hot and shock the sausage. The best method is to use a deep fryer, but a heavy deep pot will work too.

Makes 6

- 8 ¾ ounces (250 g) fresh British sausage or any mild sausage meat
- 5 ¼ ounces (150 g) ground pork
- 2 tablespoons finely chopped sage
- ⅛ teaspoon freshly grated nutmeg
- 2 tablespoons Worcestershire sauce, plus more for serving
- 1 tablespoon coarse French mustard, plus more for serving
- Salt and freshly ground black pepper
- 6 boiled 6-minute eggs (pages 9-10, cooled and peeled)
- 1 ¼ cups (150 g) all-purpose flour
- 2 eggs, beaten
- 1 ⅔ cups (100 g) breadcrumbs
- 1 ½ quarts (1 ½ l) neutral oil, for frying
- English mustard and/or Worcestershire sauce, for serving

Special equipment: food processor, deep fryer, deep-fry thermometer, and wire rack

1. Remove the sausage casings, if necessary. In the food processor, combine the sausage meat, ground pork, sage, nutmeg, Worcestershire sauce, and mustard, and process until smooth. Season to taste with salt and pepper. Chill mixture for about 30 minutes.
2. Preheat the oven to 350°F (175°C).
3. Lay a large sheet of plastic wrap on a work surface. Divide the sausage mixture into 6 balls, about 2 ½ ounces (75 g) each.
4. Place the balls on the plastic wrap and press each one to form a round patty about 6 inches (15 cm) in diameter.
5. Place an egg in the center of each patty and gently wrap the sausage mixture around the egg.
6. Arrange 3 shallow dishes next to the sausage balls. Place flour in one, beaten eggs in the second, and breadcrumbs in the third. Dip each sausage ball in flour, then in beaten egg, and finally in breadcrumbs, turning to coat evenly. Chill for at least 15 minutes or until ready to fry.
7. In a large pot or deep fryer, warm the oil to 350°F (175°C).
8. Lower the sausage balls into the oil carefully and fry for about 2 minutes, turning as needed, until golden brown all over.
9. Using a slotted spoon, remove the balls from the oil and drain on paper towels. Set the wire rack inside the baking sheet. Transfer balls to the wire rack, and bake in the center of the oven for 8-10 minutes until the sausage is fully cooked. Check with the thermometer—the sausage should be 150°F (66°C).
10. Serve warm or cold with English mustard and Worcestershire sauce.

small dishes & snacks

chorizo scotch egg

This variation on the Scotch egg leans a little Spanish with chorizo and smoked paprika.

Makes 6

1 ½ tablespoons butter

½ yellow onion, grated

½ garlic clove, finely grated

1 ½ teaspoons smoked Spanish paprika

7 ounces (200 g) fresh chorizo sausage

7 ounces (200 g) ground pork

Salt and freshly ground black pepper

6 boiled 6-minute eggs (pages 9–10), cooled and peeled

1 ¼ cups (150 g) all-purpose flour

2 eggs, beaten

1 ⅔ cups (100 g) breadcrumbs

1 ½ quarts (1 ½ l) neutral oil, for frying

Special equipment: food processor, deep fryer, deep-fry thermometer, and wire rack

1. In a skillet over medium heat, melt the butter and add the onion, garlic, and paprika. Sauté until soft.
2. Remove the sausage casing, if necessary. In the food processor, combine the sausage meat and ground pork with the sautéed onion and garlic and process until smooth. Season to taste with salt and pepper. Chill mixture for about 30 minutes.
3. Preheat the oven to 350°F (175°C).
4. Lay a large sheet of plastic wrap on a work surface. Divide the sausage mixture into 6 balls, about 2 ½ ounces (75 g) each.
5. Place the balls on the plastic wrap and press each one to form a round patty (about 6 inches/15 cm in diameter).
6. Place an egg in the center of each patty and gently wrap the sausage mixture around the egg.
7. Arrange 3 shallow dishes next to the sausage balls. Place flour in one, beaten eggs in the second, and breadcrumbs in the third. Dip each sausage ball in flour, then in beaten egg, and finally in breadcrumbs, turning to coat evenly. Chill for at least 15 minutes or until ready to fry.
8. In a large pot or deep fryer, heat the oil to 350°F (175°C).
9. Lower the sausage balls into the oil carefully and fry for about 2 minutes, turning as needed, until golden brown all over.
10. Using a slotted spoon, remove the balls from the oil and drain on paper towels. Set the wire rack inside the baking sheet. Transfer balls to the wire rack, and bake in the center of the oven for 8–10 minutes until the sausage is fully cooked. Check with the thermometer—the sausage should be 150°F (66°C).
11. Serve warm or cold.

black pudding scotch egg

Black pudding, a type of blood sausage, is quintessentially British. Though not regularly available in American grocery stores, it can be sourced online.

Makes 6

1 ½ tablespoons butter
½ yellow onion, grated
5 ¼ ounces (150 g) fresh British sausage
8 ¾ ounces (250 g) black pudding, crumbled
⅛ teaspoon ground nutmeg
2 tablespoons Worcestershire sauce
Salt and freshly ground black pepper
6 boiled 6-minute eggs (pages 9-10), cooled and peeled
1 ¼ cups (150 g) all-purpose flour
2 eggs, beaten
1 ⅔ cups (100 g) breadcrumbs
1 ½ quarts (1 ½ l) neutral oil, for frying

Special equipment: food processor, deep fryer, deep-fry thermometer, and wire rack

1. In a skillet over medium heat, melt the butter and sauté the onion until soft and lightly golden.
2. Remove the sausage casing, if necessary. In the food processor, combine the sausage meat, crumbled black pudding, sautéed onion, nutmeg, and Worcestershire sauce and process until smooth. Season to taste with salt and pepper. Chill for about 30 minutes.
3. Preheat the oven to 350°F (175°C).
4. Lay a large sheet of plastic wrap on a work surface. Divide the sausage mixture into 6 balls, about 2 ½ ounces (75 g) each.
5. Place the balls on the plastic wrap and press each one to form a round patty (about 6 inches/15 cm in diameter).
6. Place an egg in the center of each patty and gently wrap the sausage mixture around the egg.
7. Arrange 3 shallow dishes next to the sausage balls. Place flour in one, beaten eggs in the second, and breadcrumbs in the third. Dip each sausage ball in flour, then in beaten egg, and finally in breadcrumbs, turning to coat evenly. Chill for at least 15 minutes or until ready to fry.
8. In a large pot or deep fryer, heat the oil to 350°F (175°C).
9. Lower the sausage balls into the oil carefully and fry for about 2 minutes, turning as needed, until golden brown all over.
10. Using a slotted spoon, remove the balls from the oil and drain on paper towels. Set the wire rack inside the baking sheet. Transfer balls to the wire rack, and bake in the center of the oven for 8-10 minutes until the sausage is fully cooked. Check with the thermometer—the sausage should be 150°F (66°C).
11. Serve warm or cold.

potato curry scotch egg

This vegetarian version replaces the sausage and ground pork with a savory spiced potato mixture.

Makes 6

- 3 tablespoons neutral oil
- 5 ¼ ounces (150 g) leeks, thinly sliced
- 7 ounces (200 g) carrots, coarsely grated
- 2 teaspoons curry powder
- 1 teaspoon coriander seeds, crushed
- 1 teaspoon cumin seeds, crushed
- Scant ¼ cup (about 60 ml) water
- 1 pound (450 g) waxy potatoes, cooked and diced
- Salt and freshly ground black pepper
- ⅓ cup (45 g) rice flour
- 1 bunch cilantro, chopped
- 6 boiled 6-minute eggs (pages 9-10), cooled and peeled
- 1 ¼ cups (150 g) all-purpose flour
- 2 eggs, beaten
- 1 ⅔ cups (100 g) breadcrumbs
- 1 ½ quarts (1 ½ l) neutral oil, for frying
- Special equipment: food processor, deep fryer, deep-fry thermometer

1. In a large skillet over medium heat, warm the oil and sauté the leeks, carrots, curry powder, coriander, and cumin seeds. Add about ¼ cup (60 ml) water and cook, stirring, until the liquid has evaporated.
2. Add the diced potatoes to the skillet and heat through. Season to taste with salt and pepper. Transfer the mixture to a bowl and add the rice flour and cilantro. Stir to combine, then let cool.
3. Preheat the oven to 350°F (175°C).
4. Lay a large sheet of plastic wrap on a work surface. Divide the potato mixture into 6 equal balls.
5. Place the balls on the plastic wrap and press each one to form a round patty (about 6 inches (15 cm) in diameter).
6. Place an egg in the center of each patty and carefully shape the potato mixture around the egg.
7. Arrange 3 shallow dishes next to the sausage balls. Place flour in one, beaten eggs in the second, and breadcrumbs in the third. Dip each potato ball in flour, then in beaten egg, then in flour again, then in egg again, and finally in breadcrumbs, turning to coat evenly. Chill for at least 15 minutes or until ready to fry.
8. In a large pot or deep fryer, heat the oil to 350°F (175°C).
9. Lower the potato balls into the oil carefully and fry until golden brown all over, turning as needed.
10. Using a slotted spoon, remove balls from oil and drain on paper towels. Serve warm or cold.

chorizo scotch egg

black pudding scotch egg

potato curry scotch egg

chinese tea eggs

When boiled eggs are slightly cracked and left to soak in black tea and soy sauce, the final marbled look makes quite an impression.

Makes 8

8 boiled 8-minute eggs (pages 9–10) cooled
1 ½ tablespoons loose black tea
⅔ cup (160 ml) Chinese soy sauce
¼ cup (60 ml) Japanese soy sauce
3 star anise pods
1 cinnamon stick
½ teaspoon fennel seeds
½ teaspoon Sichuan peppercorns
2 cloves
1 2-inch (5-cm) piece ginger, peeled and sliced
3 tablespoons rice vinegar
2 tablespoons granulated sugar

1. Gently crack the eggshells on a hard surface or using the back of a spoon, leaving all the shell pieces on the egg.
2. In a large pot, combine 1 ½ cups (360 ml) water with the loose tea, soy sauces, star anise, cinnamon, fennel seeds, peppercorns, cloves, ginger, vinegar, and sugar. Bring to a boil. Add the eggs, reduce heat to low, and simmer for about 1 minute. Turn off the heat.
3. Using a slotted spoon, remove the eggs and transfer them to a large jar or other container with a lid. Pour the cooking liquid over the eggs. Let cool, then cover and place the container in the refrigerator.
4. Refrigerate overnight, and ideally for a few days. The eggs will keep for up to 1 week.
5. Peel to reveal the marbled pattern created by the liquid.

pickled beetroot egg

Makes 8

2 beets, peeled and cut into thick wedges

¾ cup (180 ml) white wine vinegar

½ cup (100 g) granulated sugar

2 bay leaves

5 allspice berries

½ red onion, sliced

8 boiled 11-minute eggs (pages 9–10, cooled and peeled

1. In a medium saucepan, bring 2 cups (480 ml) water to a boil. Add the beet wedges, and cook until fork-tender and the water turns red.
2. Using a slotted spoon, remove the beets and reserve for another use. Transfer 1 ¼ cups (300 ml) of the beet liquid to a large jar or other container that will fit the eggs. To the liquid, add the vinegar, sugar, bay leaves, allspice, and onion. Stir to combine, and let cool.
3. Transfer the peeled eggs to the cooled beet liquid.
4. Refrigerate overnight. The longer the eggs sit, the pinker they become. The eggs will keep for up to 1 week in the refrigerator.

small dishes & snacks

pickled dill egg

Makes 8

¾ cup (180 ml) white wine vinegar

½ cup (100 g) granulated sugar

3 bay leaves

5 allspice berries

1 ½ teaspoons mustard seeds (a mix of yellow and brown, if possible)

8 boiled 11-minute eggs (pages 9–10), cooled and peeled

2 dill sprigs

½ yellow onion, sliced

1. In a medium saucepan, combine 1 ¼ cups (300 ml) water, the vinegar, sugar, bay leaves, allspice, and mustard seeds, and bring to a boil. Let cool.
2. In a large jar or other container with a lid, layer the eggs, dill, and onion. Pour the cooled liquid over the eggs.
3. Refrigerate overnight or longer. The eggs will keep for up to 1 week in the refrigerator.

deviled eggs

Makes 4 servings

4 boiled 11-minute eggs (pages 9–10), cooled and peeled

½ cup (110 g) American-Style Whole-Egg Mayonnaise (page 39), divided

2 tablespoons finely chopped chives, divided

½ teaspoon Spanish smoked paprika, divided

⅛ teaspoon salt

Special equipment: piping bag

1. Carefully cut the eggs in half lengthwise and remove the yolks with a small spoon, transferring them to a medium bowl.
2. To the bowl with the yolks, add half the mayonnaise, and whisk until smooth. Fold in the rest of the mayonnaise, half the chives, half the paprika, and the salt.
3. Using a piping bag or spoon, pipe or spoon the yolk mixture into the egg whites. Sprinkle with the remaining chives and paprika.

small dishes & snacks

party eggs with shrimp & roe

Referred to as "Easter eggs" in Scandinavia, these gussied-up hard-boiled eggs are a Nordic tradition.

Makes 4–6 servings

1 red onion, finely chopped

2 tablespoons freshly squeezed lemon juice

⅛ teaspoon salt

6 boiled 8-minute eggs (pages 9-10), cooled and peeled

4 tablespoons crème fraîche

4 tablespoons vendace roe or other fish roe

12 small fresh shrimp, cooked and peeled

3 tablespoons microgreens

2 tablespoons fresh dill sprigs

1. In a small bowl, combine the onion, lemon juice, and salt. Let rest for at least 10 minutes.

2. Halve the eggs lengthwise and top with a dollop each of crème fraîche and roe, 2 shrimp, and a spoonful of marinated onion. Sprinkle with microgreens and dill.

small dishes & snacks

salmon rillettes with poached quail eggs

I love spreadable rillettes on toasted baguette slices. Classic rillettes are made with slow-cooked pork, but they're also commonly prepared with chicken, duck, and fish. This hot-smoked salmon is a quick, crowd-pleasing version. Simply mash the flaked fish together with crème fraîche and mayo, spread on toasted bread rounds, and top with a poached quail egg.

Makes 4-6 servings

½ cup (120 ml) white vinegar
½ cup (120 ml) cold water
10 quail eggs
7 ounces (200 g) hot-smoked salmon, flaked
2 tablespoons crème fraîche
2 tablespoons American-Style Whole-Egg Mayonnaise (page 39)
Salt
1 tablespoon olive oil
10 thin baguette slices
1-2 tablespoons finely grated horseradish
2 tablespoons finely chopped chives
Flaky sea salt

Special equipment: stand mixer fitted with the paddle attachment or hand mixer

1. In a medium bowl, combine ½ cup (120 ml) water and the vinegar. Crack the quail eggs individually into the acidic liquid and let them sit for 5 minutes.

2. Bring a large pot of water to a boil and gently slide in the quail eggs. Simmer for about 2 minutes. Remove with a slotted spoon and place in cold water.

3. Mash the salmon with a fork and then, using the mixer, mix the salmon, crème fraîche, and mayonnaise on low until combined. Season to taste with salt.

4. In a large skillet over medium heat, warm the olive oil and toast the baguette slices on both sides until golden.

5. Top each bread slice with salmon spread, a poached quail egg, horseradish, and chives. Sprinkle with flaky salt.

small dishes & snacks

avocado-baked egg

This light dish is perfect for breakfast, brunch, or lunch. Depending on the size of the avocado pit (and the egg), you might need to scoop out a bit more of the avocado to make room for the egg.

Makes 4 servings

2 ripe avocados
4 small eggs
¼ small yellow or sweet onion, finely chopped
2 tablespoons finely chopped cilantro
½ teaspoon red pepper flakes
1 tablespoon freshly squeezed lime juice
3 tablespoons olive oil
Flaky sea salt

1. Preheat the oven to 350°F (175°C) and line a baking sheet with parchment paper.
2. Halve the avocados and remove the pits. Trim a small slice off the bottom of each avocado half so they lay flat, and place them on the baking sheet.
3. Crack an egg into each avocado half.
4. Bake for about 15 minutes, until the whites are set.
5. While eggs cook, in a small bowl, combine the onion, cilantro, red pepper flakes, lime juice, and olive oil. When the avocados come out of the oven, top with the onion mixture and sprinkle with flaky sea salt.

The word *cocotte* describes a small cooking dish used in classic French cuisine; it's round, with straight sides that ensure even cooking and a creamy, pudding-like result. For this recipe, I use something similar: individual-sized ramekins. You can either crack the eggs in whole, as in the recipe, or beat them before adding to the dish for a more omelette-like consistency.

… small dishes & snacks

eggs en cocotte with tomato

Makes 4 servings

2 tablespoons olive oil
1 yellow onion, finely chopped
1 garlic clove, finely chopped
1 red bell pepper, seeded and finely chopped
1 teaspoon whole cumin seeds, crushed
1 (15-ounce/425-g) can crushed tomatoes
Salt and freshly ground black pepper
4 eggs
1 small bunch cilantro, finely chopped, for garnish
Toasted bread, for serving

Special equipment: 4 small ramekins, large high-sided baking pan big enough to hold all the ramekins

1. Preheat the oven to 400°F (200°C). Place the baking pan into the oven. Use a pitcher to pour water into the pan until it comes halfway up the sides (but not higher than the ramekins are tall).
2. In a large skillet over medium heat, warm the olive oil and sauté the onion, garlic, bell pepper, and cumin seeds until the onion is soft. Add the crushed tomatoes and ½ cup (120 ml) water, and bring to a simmer. Cook, uncovered, for about 10 minutes. Season with salt and pepper to taste.
3. Divide the sauce among the 4 ramekins. Crack an egg into each ramekin. Season with salt and pepper.
4. Cover each ramekin with foil. Carefully place them in the water bath and bake for about 10 minutes, until the whites are set but the yolks remain slightly creamy.
5. Top with cilantro and serve with the toasted bread.

eggs en cocotte with spinach

Makes 4 servings

½ tablespoon olive oil
4 ounces (120 g) fresh spinach
4 tablespoons heavy cream
4 tablespoons finely grated Parmesan cheese
4 eggs
Salt and freshly ground black pepper
2 tablespoons finely chopped chives
Toasted bread, for serving

Special equipment: 4 small ramekins, large high-sided baking pan big enough to hold all the ramekins

1. Preheat the oven to 400°F (200°C). Place the baking pan into the oven. Use a pitcher to pour water into the pan until it comes halfway up the sides (but not higher than the ramekins are tall).
2. In a large skillet over medium heat, warm the olive oil and sauté the spinach until wilted.
3. Divide the spinach among the 4 ramekins, along with the cream and Parmesan. Crack an egg into each ramekin, and season with salt and pepper.
4. Cover each ramekin with foil. Carefully place them in the water bath and bake for about 10 minutes, until the whites are set but the yolks remain slightly creamy.
5. Top with chives and a pinch each of salt and pepper, and serve with the toasted bread.

warm radishes with soft-boiled egg & five-spice pork

At the legendary Mission Chinese Food in San Francisco, I had a remarkable dish: wok-fried radishes in a hot, spicy, oil-rich sauce with five spice and crispy bits of pork belly. The beauty of the dish is that it's almost dripping with flavorful fat, which is to say, don't drain the fat from the pan. Let it remain and toss with the radishes and spinach. The combo is a true spice explosion with the rich sauce, smoky pork, and perfectly cooked egg.

Makes 4 servings

7 ounces (200 g) smoked pork belly or bacon, sliced

1 yellow onion, finely chopped

1 garlic clove, finely chopped

2 teaspoons five-spice powder

2 teaspoons raw sugar

2 ½ tablespoons white wine vinegar

2 bunches radishes, trimmed and halved

1 bunch cilantro, chopped

2 ¾ ounces (80 g) fresh spinach

Salt

4 boiled 7-minute eggs (pages 9-10)

Cooked rice, for serving

1. In a large skillet over medium-high heat, fry the pork until crispy. Add the onion, garlic, five-spice powder, and sugar toward the end of frying, and sauté a few minutes more, until the onion is soft.

2. Add the vinegar, radishes, cilantro, and spinach. Stir-fry for another minute to warm the radishes. Adjust seasoning with salt and additional vinegar if needed.

3. Crack the eggs and, using a spoon, carefully remove them from their shells. Top each serving of pork and radishes with an egg and serve with rice.

63-degree egg with vendace roe & broccoli cream

A 63-degree egg is soft and silky. I like to pair it with a vegetable purée, a bit of roe, and croutons. Sometimes, I skip the croutons and serve the dish with a piece of toast instead.

Makes 4 servings

2 tablespoons butter

2 slices sourdough bread, cubed

Salt

12 ounces (350 g) broccoli, cut into florets and stem reserved

1 teaspoon baking soda

½ cup finely chopped dill

1 ¾ ounces (50 g) butter, at room temperature

1 ½ teaspoons freshly squeezed lemon juice

¾ cup (175 g) crème fraîche

1 ¾ ounces (50 g) vendace roe or other fish roe

4 63-degree eggs (Cooking a 63-Degree Egg, page 32)

Dill sprigs, for garnish

Freshly ground black pepper

Special equipment: food processor

1. In a large skillet over medium heat, melt the butter and fry the bread cubes until crispy. Season with salt to taste and let cool.
2. Slice the broccoli stem into thin medallions and place in a bowl of ice water.
3. In a medium pot, bring 4 cups (1 l) water to a boil. Add the baking soda and 1 ½ tablespoons salt. Cook the broccoli florets until very soft. Drain.
4. In a food processor, blend the cooked broccoli, dill, and room-temperature butter until smooth. Season with the lemon juice and salt to taste. Let the purée cool; it will keep for up to 2 days in the refrigerator.
5. Strain the broccoli slices from the cold water and pat dry. Arrange in 4 shallow bowls.
6. Dollop crème fraîche, broccoli purée, and roe on top of the broccoli slices. Mix with a spoon to combine.
7. Peel the eggs, then top each dish with an egg and dill sprigs. Garnish with the bread cubes and season with salt and pepper to taste.

CLASSICS

From sandwiches and salads to tartares and Spanish tortillas, eggs play a central role in these time-honored recipes.

galette complète

Although you might be tempted to call this dish a crêpe, the French call it a galette. The distinction: buckwheat flour rather than all-purpose. This particular crispy buckwheat galette, with creamy melted cheese, smoked ham, and a runny egg yolk, is a dream. Be prepared to cook in batches if you don't have more than one crêpe pan at home.

Makes 4 galettes

Batter
1 cup (120 g) buckwheat flour
1 egg
½ teaspoon salt
2 tablespoons butter, divided

Filling
8 slices smoked ham
¾ cup (100 g) grated gruyère or comté cheese, divided
4 eggs
Salt and freshly ground black pepper
Dijon mustard, for serving

Special equipment: crêpe pan or low-sided skillet

1. Make the batter: In a medium bowl, combine the buckwheat flour with 1 ½ cups (360 ml) water. Whisk in the egg and salt. Let the batter rest for about 10 minutes.

2. Make the galettes: In the crêpe pan over medium heat, melt ½ tablespoon of butter. Pour in ¼ cup of the batter, then tilt the pan so the batter coats the pan in a thin even layer.

3. Once the galette is fully cooked on one side, about 30 seconds to 1 minute, flip it over and immediately top with 2 slices of the ham and about ¼ of the grated cheese. Create a small well in the cheese and crack in 1 egg. Fold in the edges of the galette and cook on low heat until the cheese melts and the egg sets, keeping the yolk runny. Season with salt and pepper to taste.

4. Repeat for remaining galettes, and serve immediately with Dijon mustard.

swedish "dutch baby" with pork

This dish, called an "egg cake" in Sweden, is similar to a Dutch baby, but it's cooked in a frying pan on the stovetop instead of in the oven. Egg cake hails from the county of Skåne, and, according to many, pairing it with cold-smoked pork is a must. I usually use cured pork because cold-smoked pork can be difficult to find.

Makes 4-6 servings

14 ounces (375 g) cold-smoked or cured pork belly, sliced
8 eggs
⅔ cup (80 g) all-purpose flour
1 ¼ cups (300 ml) whole milk
1 ½ cups (360 ml) heavy cream
1 teaspoon salt
2 tablespoons butter, divided
¾ cup (160 g) lingonberry preserves, for serving

1. In a large skillet over medium heat, fry the pork until crispy. Remove pork to a plate and reserve the skillet (do not wash) to use later.
2. In a large bowl, whisk together the eggs, flour, milk, cream, and salt to make a batter.
3. In the skillet over medium heat, melt 1 tablespoon of the butter. Pour in the batter.
4. As the batter begins to set, use a spatula to gently pull it in from the edges toward the center in a few spots. This allows the uncooked batter on top to flow down to the bottom of the pan and cook evenly. (This isn't about moving the cooked batter, it's about clearing paths so the raw batter can flow into the pan.)
5. Reduce the heat to low. When the batter is almost set on top, invert a plate over the skillet and flip the egg cake over onto the plate.
6. Add the remaining 1 tablespoon butter to the skillet. When it is melted, slide the Dutch baby back into the skillet. Cook until fully set.
7. Top with the pork, and serve with lingonberry preserves.

swedish steak tartare

The ideal cut for steak tartare is beef eye of round, which is lean yet still packed with flavor. While you can use tenderloin for a more luxurious dish, the eye of round is milder. If you prefer to scrape the meat instead of chopping or grinding, tenderloin is a bit easier to handle compared to the eye of round. In either case, trim the meat to remove all sinew, ensuring the tartare is smooth and tender. I grind the meat twice using the finest setting. After grinding, handle the meat gently, as overmixing can result in a sticky paste rather than a delicate tartare. To eat, you can either take a little of each ingredient on your fork, or mix everything together on the plate to create a kind of tartare mash. I prefer the latter, as it ensures you get all the flavors in every bite.

Makes 4 servings

21 ounces (600 g) trimmed beef sirloin or eye of round

4 egg yolks

Scant ½ cup (about 110 g) diced pickled beets

Scant ½ cup (about 75 g) diced pickled cucumber

1 small yellow onion, finely chopped

4 tablespoons finely grated horseradish

6 tablespoons capers

2 tablespoons Dijon mustard

Flaky sea salt and freshly ground black pepper

Special equipment: meat grinder

1. Use the meat grinder to grind the beef finely. Shape the ground meat into 4 patties (the heat from your hands can warm the meat and affect the texture, so work quickly and gently). Place the patties on plates, make a small indentation in the center of each, and place 1 egg yolk in each indentation.

2. Arrange small piles of the beets, cucumbers, onion, horseradish, capers, mustard, and salt and pepper around the patties. Serve immediately.

Tip: Make sure both the meat and the grinder are cold—put the grinder in the freezer for a short while before using it. If the equipment is too warm, the meat will become mushy when ground.

classics

steak tartare with confit egg yolk

Confiting creates the creamiest egg yolk imaginable. While you might be more familiar with confited duck, cooking egg yolks submerged in oil over low heat yields a creamy, almost mayonnaise-y egg, without any added oil.

Makes 4 servings

1 ¾ cups (420 ml) neutral oil

6 egg yolks

21 ounces (600 g) trimmed veal, beef sirloin, or eye of round

4 shallots, finely chopped

4 tablespoons Dijon mustard, divided

3 tablespoons coarsely chopped capers

3 tablespoons finely chopped cornichons

2 tablespoons finely chopped chives

3 tablespoons microgreens

3 tablespoons chopped shiso or Thai basil

2 tablespoons grassy, peppery olive oil

Flaky sea salt and freshly ground black pepper

Special equipment: meat grinder, piping bag (optional)

1. Preheat the oven to 170°F (75°C).
2. Pour the oil into a small ovenproof dish or pot and add the egg yolks; they should be submerged. If not, add a bit more oil.
3. Bake in the middle of the oven for 45 minutes.
4. Using a slotted spoon, remove the yolks to a bowl and let cool.
5. Whisk the yolks into a creamy consistency. If you wish, transfer to a piping bag.
6. Use the meat grinder to grind the beef finely. Transfer meat to a bowl, and, working quickly, add the shallots, 2 tablespoons of the mustard, the capers, and cornichons. Form into 4 patties, and place the patties on plates.
7. Pipe or dollop the egg cream over the patties and garnish with chives, microgreens, and shiso or basil.
8. Drizzle olive oil over each patty and dollop the remaining 2 tablespoons of mustard on the plates. Season to taste with salt and pepper.

italian steak tartare

Grocery stores and specialty markets stock an abundance of sun-dried tomatoes, olives and capers on their shelves. Choose high-quality ingredients for this recipe; they'll make the whole dish.

If using high-quality veal, rather than grinding it, you can scrape the meat with a sharp knife to achieve a silky, melt-in-your-mouth tartare. This method takes a bit longer but is absolutely worth it. Just be sure to keep the meat cold—divide it into pieces, scrape one piece at a time, and keep the remainder in the refrigerator until ready to use.

Makes 4 servings

21 ounces (600 g) trimmed veal, beef sirloin, or eye of round

4 egg yolks

3 tablespoons finely chopped sun-dried tomatoes

1 small red onion, finely chopped

6 tablespoons capers

4 anchovy fillets, finely chopped

3 tablespoons black olives (preferably Taggiasca or kalamata), finely chopped

2 tablespoons finely chopped parsley

2 tablespoons finely chopped basil

4 tablespoons grassy and peppery olive oil

1 ounce (30 g) finely grated Parmesan

Flaky sea salt and freshly ground black pepper

Dijon mustard (optional)

Special equipment: meat grinder

1. Use the meat grinder to grind the beef finely. Shape the ground meat into 4 patties (the heat from your hands can warm the meat and affect the texture, so work quickly and gently).

2. Place the patties on plates, make a small indentation in the center of each, and place 1 egg yolk in each indentation.

3. Around the patties, arrange the sun-dried tomatoes, onion, capers, anchovies, olives, parsley, and basil. Drizzle with olive oil and top with Parmesan. Serve with salt and pepper (be mindful that the accompaniments add a lot of salt, so you may not need much more, but you should add plenty of pepper to give the dish its kick). If you want some heat, add a dollop of Dijon mustard, though it's not traditionally Italian.

asian beef tartare with gochujang mayonnaise

This tartare has a bolder flavor because it's made with ribeye instead of the leaner eye of round or tenderloin. Ribeye has a good amount of marbling, which adds a rich, beefy taste. Trim off some of the thicker fat, but keep the rest for flavor. It's crucial that both the grinder and the meat are very cold, or the fat may melt from the friction in the grinder, turning the meat into a greasy mess.

Makes 4 servings

1 red onion, thinly sliced into rings
2 tablespoons all-purpose flour
½ teaspoon baking powder
¼ teaspoon salt
Neutral oil, for frying and for mayonnaise
2 egg yolks
gochujang paste
21 ounces (600 g) trimmed ribeye or eye of round
1 tablespoon soy sauce
1 teaspoon sesame oil
1 teaspoon finely grated fresh ginger
2 tablespoons sesame seeds, toasted and cooled
2 tablespoons Sriracha
1 tablespoon rice vinegar
3 tablespoons microgreens
6 tablespoons shiso cress or small leaves from 1 bunch Thai basil
Flaky sea salt and freshly ground black pepper

Special equipment: deep-fry thermometer, meat grinder

1. Separate the onion slices into rings.
2. In a medium bowl, combine the flour, baking powder, and salt.
3. Lightly moisten the onion rings with water, then add them to the flour mixture and toss to coat.
4. Add neutral oil to a large pot or deep fryer. Heat the oil to 360°F (180°C) and fry the onion rings until golden and crispy. Remove from oil and let them drain on paper towels.
5. Make a basic mayonnaise from the egg yolks and ¾ cup + 1 tablespoon + 1 teaspoon of the neutral oil (Mayonnaise, page 39). Stir in gochujang paste to taste.
6. Use the meat grinder to grind the beef finely. Transfer meat to a bowl, and, working quickly, stir in the soy sauce, sesame oil, and grated ginger.
7. Shape the mixture into 4 patties. Roll the edges in the toasted sesame seeds and place on plates.
8. In a small bowl, combine the Sriracha and rice vinegar.
9. Top the patties with a dollop of gochujang mayo. Drizzle the Sriracha-vinegar sauce around the edge of the plate. Scatter onion rings, any remaining sesame seeds, the microgreens, and shisho cress on and around the patties. Season to taste with flaky salt and pepper.

swedish toast with tenderloin, roe, and egg

This classic dish (called *pelle janzon* in Swedish) features thinly pounded beef tenderloin on toast with an egg and vendace roe. It's a Swedish delicacy sometimes called "Nordic caviar." The Swedish opera singer Per Janzon is said to have enjoyed this luxurious dish frequently in the late 1800s. You can either pound the tenderloin yourself using a meat mallet or ask your butcher to do it for you. The original recipe doesn't include horseradish, but I find it adds that extra little kick.

A traditional *pelle janzon* calls for paper-thin, almost transparent slices of beef without marbling. I, however, prefer the tenderloin to have some marbling, as it enhances the flavor of the meat. It can be a bit trickier to pound marbled meat thin, as the fat tends to tear. It may not look as neat, but the flavor is worth it.

Makes 6 servings

6 slices white bread
3 ½ tablespoons butter
6 slices beef tenderloin, about 1 ¾ ounces (50 g) each
3 ½ ounces (100 g) roe, ideally vendace or lumpfish
6 quail eggs
2 tablespoons finely chopped chives
1 red onion, finely chopped
1 tablespoon finely grated horseradish
Flaky sea salt and freshly ground black pepper

1. Trim the edges of the bread slices to create small squares about 1 ½ inches (4 cm) on each side.
2. In a large skillet over medium heat, melt the butter and fry the bread on both sides until golden brown and crispy. Set aside on a plate.
3. Place the beef slices between two pieces of plastic wrap or in a resealable plastic bag. Pound until very thin (1–2 mm).
4. Place 1 pounded tenderloin on each piece of toast. Top each toast with a spoonful of roe, and create a small indentation in the center of each spoonful (for the quail egg yolk).
5. Carefully cut the shells of the quail eggs and separate the yolks from the whites. Reserve the whites for another use, and carefully place each yolk in the indentation in the roe.
6. Top each serving with chives, onion, and horseradish. Season to taste with salt and pepper.

veal tartare with tarragon, anchovy mayo, and fried capers

To balance the richness of this dish, it's great to serve it with crispy, salty capers. Before frying, be sure to place the capers on a paper towel to dry them—otherwise, they'll splatter in the oil.

Just as with steak tartare or other raw dishes, it's essential to keep the meat cold throughout preparation. Take out a small portion at a time to chop, and then return it to the refrigerator until ready to serve, as the meat quickly reaches room temperature on the plate. Choose high-quality meat, such as a flavorful farm-raised cut with a bit of marbling.

Makes 4 servings

1 egg yolk

1 tablespoon white wine vinegar

2 tablespoons finely chopped tarragon, plus tarragon leaves, for garnish

1 anchovy fillet, finely chopped

Neutral oil, for mayonnaise and frying

2 tablespoons coarse French mustard

Salt

¼ cup (60 g) capers, dried

1 pound (500 g) veal or beef sirloin, sliced and then finely diced (refrigerate until serving)

4 quail egg yolks

1 ½ tablespoons finely chopped chives

Freshly ground black pepper

Thinly sliced toasted bread, for serving

Special equipment: deep-fry thermometer

1. In a medium bowl, combine the egg yolk, vinegar, tarragon, and anchovy. Gradually whisk in ⅔ cup (160 ml) of the oil until a thick mayonnaise forms. Stir in the mustard, season to taste with salt, and adjust with more vinegar if needed.

2. In a small pot, heat ¾ cup (180 ml) oil to 350°F (175°C). Add the capers to the oil and fry until the buds open and turn crispy, about 3–4 minutes. Remove with a slotted spoon and drain on paper towels.

3. Divide the meat between 4 plates. Top each portion with 1 quail egg yolk, a few dollops of tarragon mayo, fried capers, chives, and tarragon leaves. Season with salt and pepper.

4. Serve with the toasted bread.

Tip: Try swapping out the veal for fresh tuna or salmon for a lighter version of the tartare.

The *Parisersmörgås* has been a part of Swedish cuisine since the early 1920s, when it was commonly served in restaurants all over the country. Originally, it was likely a type of "hash-on-toast" dish, as it could include just about anything. Over time, it evolved into an open-faced sandwich topped with a seasoned ground beef patty mixed with chopped beets, capers, and pickled cucumbers. It's always topped with a fried egg.

parisermacka

parisian sandwich

Makes 2 servings

5 ½ tablespoons butter, divided, plus more for the eggs

2 slices white bread (preferably sourdough)

10 ½ ounces (300 g) ground beef or veal

3 tablespoons finely diced pickled beets, divided

1 small yellow onion, finely chopped, divided

Salt and freshly ground black pepper

2 tablespoons cream cheese

1 tablespoon coarse-grain Swedish or brown mustard

½ tablespoon Dijon mustard

3 tablespoons capers

3 tablespoons finely chopped cornichons

½ tablespoon white wine vinegar

2 tablespoons finely chopped parsley

2 eggs

1. In a large skillet over medium heat, melt 1 tablespoon of the butter and toast the bread on both sides until golden. Place on two plates, and set the skillet aside.

2. In a large bowl, combine the ground meat, 1 ½ tablespoons pickled beets, and half the chopped onion. Season to taste with salt and pepper, and shape the mixture into 2 patties.

3. In the skillet over medium heat, melt 1 tablespoon of the butter. Add the patties and cook for about 5 minutes on each side, until they get a deep browned surface. (I prefer mine well-browned, almost to the point of being slightly charred.)

4. In a small bowl, stir together the cream cheese and both mustards. Spread this mixture on the toast slices.

5. Top each toast with capers, cornichons, the remaining beets and onions, and 1 fried patty.

6. In a saucepan over medium-low heat, melt the remaining 3 ½ tablespoons butter and cook until it turns golden and has a nutty aroma. Remove from the heat and allow the browned bits to settle at the bottom. Leaving the milk solids behind, pour the browned butter into a clean pan, reheat, and stir in the vinegar and parsley. Keep warm until serving.

7. Fry the eggs sunny-side up (Classic French Fried Egg, page 14).

8. Place the eggs on top of the patties. Drizzle with the browned butter and serve.

swedish hash

Prefer a vegetarian version? Dice some tofu, another plant-based protein, or halloumi and toss it into the mix instead of the meat. Add extra browned onions and a dash of smoked paprika for an added depth of flavor.

Makes 4 servings

8 large waxy potatoes, peeled
Salt
7 tablespoons butter, divided
Freshly ground black pepper
2 yellow onions, finely chopped
5 ounces (150 g) smoked pork belly, diced
9 ounces (250 g) Swedish sausage or pork sausage, diced
4 eggs
10 ½ ounces (300 g) beef tenderloin, diced
2 tablespoons finely chopped parsley
Pickled beets, cornichons, ketchup, mustard, and/or HP sauce, for serving (Homemade Ketchup, Homemade Mustard, and Brown Sauce HP-Style, pages 78-79)

1. In a large pot, cover the potatoes with salted water and bring to a boil. Parboil until a knife inserted in a potato meets slight resistance. Drain the potatoes, and, when cool enough to handle, dice into ½ -inch (1.25-cm) pieces.

2. In a large skillet over medium-high heat, melt 3 tablespoons of the butter. Add the diced potatoes and fry, turning occasionally, for 10 minutes or until they get crispy and golden brown. Set aside on a plate or tray. Season to taste with salt and pepper.

3. In the same skillet over medium heat, melt 2 more tablespoons of the butter and add the onions and a pinch of salt. Sauté for about 5 minutes, until they turn light brown and soft. Use a slotted spoon to transfer the onions to the plate with the potatoes.

4. In the same skillet over medium heat, fry the pork and sausage for about 10 minutes, until well browned. If needed, strain off excess fat. Add the pork and sausage to the plate with the potatoes and onions. Set the skillet aside to use for the beef.

5. In a separate large skillet over medium heat, melt 1 more tablespoon of the butter and fry the eggs until their bottoms are golden and crispy.

6. In the original skillet over medium-high heat, melt the remaining 1 tablespoon of butter and add the beef. Sear on all sides for about 3 minutes, to medium rare. Return the potatoes, onions, pork, and sausage to the pan, stir to combine, and reduce heat to low to warm everything through.

7. Top with fried egg and sprinkle with parsley. Serve with beets, cornichons, ketchup, mustard, and HP sauce.

swedish beef & potatoes

Hotel Rydberg, located at Gustav Adolf's Square in Stockholm, was the place to let loose during the late 1800s and early 1900s; creatives like Albert Engström and Hjalmar Söderberg could be found there enjoying food and drinks in good company late into the night. The hotel was demolished in 1914, but its legacy lives on through this elevated version of hash with beef tenderloin and mustard cream. The trick is to get the large cubed potatoes perfectly crispy. The secret, of course, is butter.

Makes 4 servings

7 tablespoons butter, divided

4 tablespoons neutral oil

8 large waxy potatoes, peeled and diced into ¾-inch (2-cm) pieces

Salt and freshly ground black pepper

4 tablespoons finely chopped flat-leaf parsley

3 yellow onions, chopped

⅔ cup (160 g) crème fraîche

3 tablespoons coarse-grain Swedish or brown mustard

3 tablespoons finely grated horseradish, plus more for garnish (optional)

25 ounces (700 g) beef tenderloin, cut into 1 ¼-inch (3-cm) dice

4 egg yolks

Special equipment: hand mixer

1. Preheat the oven to 210°F (100°C).

2. In a large skillet over medium heat, melt 3 ½ tablespoons of the butter and add 2 tablespoons of the oil. Add the potatoes and fry over medium heat for about 20 minutes until golden, crispy, and fully cooked through. Season to taste with salt and pepper. Transfer to a baking sheet and toss with the parsley. Place the baking sheet in the oven to keep warm.

3. In the same skillet over medium heat, melt 1 more tablespoon of the butter and add 1 more tablespoon of the oil. Add the onions and a pinch of salt, and sauté for about 10 minutes, until the onions are soft and golden brown. Transfer the onions to the tray with the potatoes in the oven.

4. Place the crème fraîche in a medium bowl and use the mixer to whip until fluffy. Add the mustard and horseradish, and whip to combine. Refrigerate the mustard cream until serving.

5. Return the skillet to medium heat and add the remaining 2 ½ tablespoons butter and 1 tablespoon oil. When sizzling, add the beef to the pan, season with salt and pepper, and fry for 1 minute on each side, without moving the pieces, to achieve a good sear.

6. Divide the beef between 4 plates and top with potatoes and onions. Add an egg yolk and a dollop of mustard cream to each plate. Serve immediately, garnished with additional grated horseradish if desired.

The Spanish tortilla is cooked in a pan with an abundance of olive oil and should have a slightly runny interior when served. In contrast, the Italian frittata is baked in the oven, often on a tray, and is served firm, almost like a crustless quiche.

spanish tortilla

… classics …

spanish tortilla

Makes 6–8 servings

⅔ cup (160 ml) olive oil
21 ounces (600 g) waxy potatoes, peeled and cut into ¾-inch (2-cm) dice
2 yellow onions, finely chopped
1 green or red bell pepper, seeded and diced
Salt and freshly ground black pepper
6 eggs
½ teaspoon chopped, fresh parsley

1. In a deep-sided pan over medium heat, warm the olive oil and fry the potatoes for about 10 minutes, turning occasionally. Add the onions and bell pepper, then reduce heat to low and cook for another 10 minutes. Season with salt and pepper. Let cool slightly.
2. In a large bowl, beat the eggs with a little salt and pepper. Use a slotted spoon to transfer the potatoes, onions, and bell pepper to the bowl, leaving the oil behind in the pan. Stir to mix the eggs and vegetables.
3. Reserve 4 tablespoons of oil from the pan, and discard the rest.
4. In a large skillet over medium heat, warm 2 tablespoons of the reserved oil, and then pour in the egg, veggie, and potato mixture. Cook without stirring for 5 minutes.
5. Loosen the edges of the tortilla with a spatula, invert a plate over the skillet, and carefully flip the tortilla onto the plate.
6. Return the skillet to medium heat and add the remaining 2 tablespoons of reserved oil. Slide the tortilla back into the pan, uncooked side down, and cook for 5 minutes. (For a firmer center, extend cooking time to 7 or 8 minutes.)
7. Let the tortilla rest for at least 5 minutes before serving. Sprinkle on the fresh parsley and serve warm or at room temperature. The inside should be slightly runny.

italian frittata

Makes 4–6 servings

3 tablespoons olive oil, divided
½ zucchini, thinly sliced
1 red bell pepper, seeded and thinly sliced
Salt and freshly ground black pepper
3 ½ ounces (100 g) fresh spinach leaves
¼ cup small basil leaves
4 ½ ounces (125 g) mozzarella, torn into pieces
1 ¾ ounces (50 g) finely grated Parmesan
8 eggs
1 red onion, thinly sliced

Special equipment: 10 x 10-inch (25 x 25-cm) baking dish

1. Preheat the oven to 350°F (175°C).
2. In a large skillet over medium heat, warm 2 tablespoons of the olive oil. Add the zucchini and bell pepper and sauté for about 10 minutes until they soften and lose excess moisture. Season to taste with salt and pepper, then transfer to the baking dish.
3. In the skillet over medium heat, warm the remaining 1 tablespoon oil and add the spinach. Stir until wilted, then add to the dish with the zucchini and pepper. Stir in the basil.
4. Scatter the mozzarella and Parmesan over the vegetables.
5. In a medium bowl, beat the eggs. Pour the eggs over the vegetables and cheese. Top with red onion and season to taste with salt and pepper.
6. Bake in the center of the oven for about 25 minutes, until the frittata is set. Sprinkle with parsley then serve.

classics

niçoise salad

This classic French salad is perfect for summer heat. Anchovies, olives, and capers bring a briny punch that's balanced with bright lemon and crisp greens. For the best flavor, choose tuna in olive oil.

Makes 4 servings

14 ounces (400 g) boiled potatoes, preferably new or small waxy potatoes

Salt

5 ounces (150 g) haricots verts (green beans)

1 ½ teaspoons Dijon mustard

1 tablespoon red wine vinegar

1 tablespoon freshly squeezed lemon juice

1 teaspoon honey or granulated sugar

Flaky salt

3 tablespoons olive oil

1 red onion, very thinly sliced

1 head of lettuce (preferably gem or butterhead)

7 ounces (200 g) cherry tomatoes, halved

8 anchovy fillets (optional)

4 tablespoons capers

½ cup (70 g) small black olives, preferably taggiasca or kalamata

2 cans tuna in olive oil, drained

2-4 boiled 7-minute eggs (pages 9-10), peeled and quartered

Freshly ground black pepper

Lemon wedges, for serving

1. In a medium pot, cover the potatoes with salted water. Bring to a boil and cook until potatoes are tender. Drain and let cool.

2. Bring another medium pot of salted water to a boil and add the haricots verts. Boil for 3 minutes, until crisp-tender, then drain and rinse under ice-cold water. Strain the haricots and lay them on kitchen towels to dry.

3. In a large bowl, make the dressing: whisk together the Dijon mustard, vinegar, lemon juice, honey, a pinch of flaky salt, and olive oil.

4. Add the red onion to the dressing and let sit for about 10 minutes.

5. Toss the potatoes and haricots verts in the dressing.

6. Separate the lettuce leaves and add them to the bowl along with the tomatoes, anchovy fillets, capers, and olives. Break the tuna into chunks and fold in gently. Transfer to a serving platter, and top with the boiled eggs.

7. Season to taste with salt and pepper and serve with lemon wedges.

egg and anchovy tartare

Makes 4 servings

3 tablespoons diced pickled beets

4 egg yolks

1 (4 ½-ounce/125-g) tin anchovies, drained and chopped

4 tablespoons finely chopped flat-leaf parsley

1 small red onion, finely chopped

Scant ½ cup (about 70 g) diced cornichons

4 tablespoons capers

Crispbread, for serving

Butter, for serving

Västerbotten cheese, for serving

1. Place piles of the diced beets in the center of 4 plates. Top each beet pile with an egg yolk.
2. Arrange the anchovies, parsley, onions, cornichons, and capers around the beets like a wreath.
3. Mix everything together on the plate before eating. Serve with crispbread, butter, and, if desired, a slice of cheese.

Tip: I never tire of this eggy, mayo-creamy, and sweet-salty anchovy mixture served on crispy crispbread. There are countless variations of this salad (called gubbröra in Swedish)—sometimes made with caviar instead of vendace roe, sometimes without potatoes, sometimes with herring instead of anchovies, and sometimes with crème fraîche instead of mayo. But my version is the ultimate recipe.

egg and anchovy salad

Makes 4–6 servings

4 boiled 9-minute eggs (pages 9-10), peeled and chopped

2 small boiled potatoes, finely diced

⅓ yellow onion, finely chopped

3 tablespoons mayonnaise (page 39)

1 (4 ½-ounce/125-g) tin anchovies, drained and chopped

3 tablespoons vendace roe or other fish roe

1 tablespoon finely chopped chives

½ tablespoon finely chopped dill

Crispbread, for serving

1. Transfer the eggs to a large bowl.
2. Mix in the potatoes, onion, and mayonnaise.
3. Fold in the anchovies, roe, chives, and dill.
4. Serve with crispbread.

lyonnaise salad

If you can't find frisée, try mixing finely sliced endive with iceberg lettuce to achieve a similar bitterness and crunch. Bitterness is essential to this dish and, combined with crispy pork belly, poached eggs, Dijon mustard, and honey, it creates a perfectly balanced flavor experience. Note: In a pinch, you can sub thick-cut bacon for the pork belly.

Makes 4 servings

1 head frisée lettuce
1 garlic clove, peeled
8 ounces (225 g) pork belly
1 ½ tablespoons Dijon mustard
2 tablespoons white wine vinegar
½ tablespoon honey
4 tablespoons olive oil
6 tablespoons capers
Flaky sea salt and freshly ground black pepper
4 poached eggs (Classic Poached Eggs, page 18)

1. Soak the frisée in ice-cold water.
2. In a small saucepan, cover the garlic clove with water and bring to a boil. Simmer for about 10 minutes, until soft.
3. Remove the skin from the pork belly and cut into strips. In a medium dry skillet over medium heat, pan-fry until crispy. Drain on paper towels.
4. In a medium bowl, mash the cooked garlic and whisk in the mustard, vinegar, 1 tablespoon water, and honey. Slowly whisk in olive oil to create a creamy dressing.
5. Remove the frisée from the water, shake dry, and discard the outer leaves.
6. Tear the remaining leaves, add to a large bowl, and toss with the dressing.
7. Arrange the frisée on plates, layering with pork belly and capers. Season with salt and pepper. Top each plate with a poached egg.

Mains

Eggs are so versatile that they often form the backbone (sometimes obviously, sometimes not) of these dishes.

There's a reason why this ever-popular pasta dish has its name: it should be loaded with black pepper—black like coal (*carbone* in Italian). The classic version doesn't include cream or onions; it's the egg yolk that creates the creamy, flavorful sauce. But if you're craving a creamier carbonara with a bit more depth, add a tablespoon of cream when the pasta is tossed with the sautéed onions, egg yolk, and guanciale. I've taken a couple more liberties: carbonara is usually made with spaghetti, but I make it with tagliatelle. I also like to serve the dish topped with a raw egg yolk, instead of incorporating all the yolks into the sauce.

carbonara

carbonara

Makes 4 servings

3 tablespoons olive oil, divided

7 ounces (200 g) guanciale, pancetta, or smoked pork belly, diced

2 yellow onions, finely chopped (optional)

Salt

1 recipe Egg Pasta, cut into tagliatelle (see below)

6 egg yolks, divided

3 ½ ounces (100 g) finely grated Parmesan, divided

Freshly ground black pepper

1. In a medium skillet over medium heat, warm 1 tablespoon of the olive oil and add the guanciale. Cook until crisp, then set aside on paper towels to drain.

2. In a large skillet over low heat, warm the remaining 2 tablespoons of olive oil and sauté the onions for about 10 minutes, until very soft and sweet. (If you wish to keep the recipe traditional, omit the onions.) Set the skillet aside with the onions in it.

3. Bring a large pot of salted water to a boil. Add the pasta, and cook until al dente, about 3 minutes. Drain and transfer to the skillet with the onions. Add the guanciale, 2 egg yolks, and half of the Parmesan, and quickly toss to coat in the skillet.

4. Serve the pasta on plates, topping with the remaining Parmesan, salt, plenty of black pepper, and 1 egg yolk per plate. Direct diners to mix the egg yolk with the pasta to make a creamier sauce.

egg pasta

Makes 6 servings

1 ¼ cups (160 g) durum wheat flour, plus more for dusting

1 ¼ cups (145 g) 00 flour

3 whole eggs

4 egg yolks

Special equipment: pasta machine (optional)

1. In a medium bowl, combine and thoroughly mix the durum flour and 00 flour and, on a clean work surface, pour the flour into a mound. Create a well in the center of the flour and crack in the eggs and yolks. Using a fork, mix the eggs with the flour until a crumbly dough forms. Add a little water (about 1 tablespoon) if needed, and knead until smooth and elastic.

2. Wrap the dough in plastic and let rest in the refrigerator for about 1 hour.

3. Use a pasta machine to roll out and shape the dough as desired, dusting with durum flour as necessary. Cook immediately (by boiling in salted water for about 3 minutes) or allow to dry before storing in an airtight container.

Tip: Use durum wheat flour to dust the pasta while working, which prevents the dough from sticking to the machine or the countertop. If you don't have a pasta machine, you can roll out the dough by hand–just like a true Italian *nonna*. It's more work, but it gives an authentic Italian pasta-making experience.

pasta with sausage & egg

The beauty of using egg yolk in pasta dishes with cream or broth is that the egg binds with the starch from the pasta, creating a creamy sauce without needing any flour as a thickener. For this dish, you'll want to use pappardelle. To make the pasta by hand, roll the dough thin using a pasta machine, then cut it by hand into wide ribbons, about 1 inch (2-3 cm) thick. Of course, you can also roll out the dough by hand.

Makes 4 servings

2 tablespoons olive oil, divided

14 ounces (400 g) Italian sausage, roughly chopped

½ leek, chopped

1 garlic clove, finely chopped

½ teaspoon whole fennel seeds, crushed

⅔ cup (160 ml) dry white wine

¾ cup (180 ml) heavy cream

Salt

1 recipe Egg Pasta, cut into pappardelle (page 139)

6 egg yolks, divided

Scant ½ cup (30 g) finely chopped herbs (such as parsley, thyme, rosemary, and sage)

⅓ cup (50 g) grated Grana Padano cheese, divided

Freshly ground black pepper

1. In a medium skillet over medium heat, warm 1 tablespoon of the olive oil and add the sausage. Fry for 10 minutes, then remove to a plate and set aside. Wipe out the skillet.

2. Return the skillet to medium heat and warm the remaining 1 tablespoon olive oil. Add the leek, garlic, and fennel seeds. Sauté for 5 minutes, then add the wine and cook, stirring, until reduced by half. Add the cream and let simmer for 5 minutes. Remove from the heat.

3. Bring a large pot of salted water to boil. Add the pasta, and cook until al dente, about 2-3 minutes. Drain and transfer to the skillet with the cream sauce. Add the sausage, 2 of the egg yolks, the herbs, and half the Grana Padano, and toss until the sauce becomes creamy and coats the pasta. Season with salt and pepper to taste.

4. Serve the pasta on plates, topping with the remaining Grana Padano and 1 egg yolk per plate.

mains

ravioli with ricotta & quail eggs

If you're short on time and can't make your own pasta dough, you can use premade gyoza wrappers instead. While not an exact replica for pasta dough, gyoza wrappers are already shaped into circles and easy to work with. The dough is very thin, so it requires only a short cooking time.

Makes 4 servings (about 4 ravioli per person)

Salt

1 garlic clove

1 (8-ounce/250-g) container ricotta cheese

¼ cup (28 g) finely grated Parmesan, plus more for garnish

¼ cup (21 g) finely chopped chives

2 tablespoons finely chopped thyme

Zest of ½ lemon

Ground coriander

Freshly ground black pepper

1 recipe Egg Pasta (page 139), rolled very thin and cut into 2 4-inch (10-cm) wide strips, or 1 12-ounce (340 g) package gyoza wrappers, thawed if necessary

16 quail egg yolks

4 tablespoons olive oil

1 small bunch basil, leaves julienned

Flaky salt, for garnish

Special equipment: piping bag

1. Bring a small pot of salted water to a boil. Blanch the garlic in the boiling water for about 5 minutes. Remove and finely grate garlic into a medium bowl.

2. To the bowl with the garlic, add the ricotta, Parmesan, chives, thyme, lemon zest, and 2 pinches of coriander. Season with salt and pepper to taste. Transfer the filling to the piping bag.

3. Place the pasta strips or gyoza wrappers on a work surface. Pipe out mounds of about 2 tablespoons of filling. If using pasta strips, leave 1 ¼–1 ½ inches (3–4 cm) of space between mounds. Repeat until you have piped 16 mounds.

4. Make a small well in each mound and add a quail egg yolk. Cover with another strip of pasta or more gyoza wrappers, pressing gently around the filling to remove air bubbles.

5. Use the rim of a glass or a round cookie cutter to cut out the ravioli. Seal the edges with a fork. (Any pasta scraps can be cut into tagliatelle and cooked.)

6. Bring a large pot of salted water to a boil, and add the ravioli. Cook for about 3-4 minutes, until al dente. Drain and serve immediately with olive oil, basil, and a little grated Parmesan. Sprinkle to taste with flaky sea salt and black pepper.

polenta with mushrooms & egg

"I ate the polenta and suddenly found myself in an entirely new place. Like for many first-time polenta eaters, my world transformed from dull and gray to sunny and bright yellow." –*Bill Buford*

When I devoured the book *Heat* by Bill Buford, polenta took on new meaning for me. In one chapter, he dives deep into making the very best polenta. This creamy dish served with a soft-boiled egg and crispy sautéed mushrooms is my attempt to do the same.

Makes 4 servings

- 3 ¾ cups (900 ml) chicken broth
- ½ cup (120 ml) dry white wine
- ½ cup (80 g) polenta
- 1 tablespoon finely chopped fresh thyme
- 1 tablespoon finely chopped fresh chives
- ½ cup (120 ml) heavy cream
- 4 eggs
- 2 tablespoons butter, divided
- 9 ounces (250 g) mixed mushrooms, such as shiitake, trumpet, or portobello, sliced
- 1 garlic clove, finely chopped
- Salt and freshly ground black pepper
- 5 ounces (140 g) fresh spinach
- 2 ounces (60 g) Parmesan, finely grated
- ¼ teaspoon white truffle oil

1. In a large saucepan, combine the broth and wine and bring to a boil.
2. Whisk in the polenta and reduce heat to low. Add the thyme and chives.
3. Let the polenta simmer gently, uncovered, for 1 hour. Stir occasionally—but not too often, as polenta prefers to be left alone. Add more broth or water if it becomes too thick.
4. Stir in the cream and let simmer for another 15 minutes. The polenta should be creamy and slightly runny.
5. Bring a medium pot of water to a boil. Lower the eggs into the water, lower the heat, and simmer for 5 minutes.
6. Drain and rinse the eggs briefly in cold water—just enough to stop the cooking, not cool them completely. Peel the eggs and set aside.
7. In a large skillet over medium heat, melt 1 tablespoon of the butter and add the mushrooms and garlic. Sauté until golden. Season with salt and pepper. Transfer the mushrooms to a plate and, in the same skillet over medium heat, sauté the spinach until wilted. Season with salt and pepper.
8. Remove the polenta from the heat. Stir in the Parmesan, remaining 1 tablespoon butter, and truffle oil. Season to taste with salt and pepper.
9. Spoon the polenta onto plates and top with the sautéed mushrooms, spinach, and one soft-boiled egg per serving.

steak hash

This is the American diner and steakhouse version of the Swedish hashbrown dish *pyttipanna*. The key difference is that it should be extra hearty, with mashed-up potato pieces mixed in. Go for a top-quality steak with plenty of marbling for the best flavor.

Makes 4 servings

1 ¾ pounds (800 g) waxy potatoes, peeled
Salt
7 tablespoons butter, divided
2 yellow onions, finely chopped
3 celery stalks, sliced
1 pound (500 g) beef ribeye, cut into ¾-inch (2-cm) cubes
Freshly ground black pepper
2 tablespoons chili sauce
½ teaspoon Tabasco sauce
2 teaspoons Worcestershire sauce
2 teaspoons finely chopped rosemary
4 tablespoons finely chopped parsley
8 small or 4 large eggs

1. In a large pot, cover the potatoes with salted water and bring to a boil. Cook until tender, then drain and let cool slightly before cutting into ¾-inch (2-cm) cubes. Place on a large plate.

2. In a large skillet over low heat, melt 2 tablespoons butter and sauté the onions and celery for 10 minutes. Transfer to the plate with the potatoes.

3. In the same skillet over medium heat, melt 1 tablespoon butter and add the beef. Fry for 3 minutes. Season to taste with salt and pepper.

4. To the skillet, add the potatoes, onions, celery, chili sauce, Tabasco, Worcestershire sauce, rosemary, and parsley. Cook together over medium heat for about 5 minutes. Let the hash sit in the pan without stirring to allow the potatoes on the bottom to become crispy.

5. In a medium skillet over medium heat, melt 1 tablespoon butter. If using 8 small eggs, crack 2 into a bowl, then slide the eggs into the skillet together. If using 4 large eggs, cook them individually. Either way, cook them sunny-side up (Classic French Fried Egg, page 14). Repeat until all eggs are cooked. Season to taste with salt and pepper.

6. Taste and adjust the seasoning of the hash. Divide between plates, and serve with the fried eggs on top and extra chili sauce on the side.

pickled herring with 65-degree eggs & brown butter

This is my tribute to pickled herring, eggs, and browned butter. For a Scandinavian, there's nothing better to enjoy on a warm summer day, along with an ice-cold beer.

Makes 4 servings

Salt
1 pound (500 g) new potatoes
½ cucumber, thinly sliced
1 tablespoon granulated sugar
½ tablespoon white vinegar
10 radishes, thinly sliced
⅔ cup (85 g) all-purpose flour
1 ½ teaspoons baking powder
8 shallots, sliced into thin rings
1 ¼ cups (300 ml) neutral oil, for frying
3 ½ ounces (100 g) butter
4 65-degree eggs (63-, 64- & 65-Degree Eggs, page 32)
2 7-ounce (200 g) cans pickled herring fillets
1 red onion, very thinly sliced
⅔ cup (135 g) sour cream or crème fraîche
2 tablespoons finely chopped chives
3 tablespoons microgreens
¼ cup fresh dill sprigs
1 tablespoon finely grated horseradish
Flaky sea salt

Special equipment: deep-fry thermometer

1. Bring a large pot of salted water to a boil. Add the new potatoes and cook until tender. Drain and set aside to cool.
2. While potatoes cook, in a medium bowl, combine the cucumber, sugar, vinegar, 1 ½ tablespoons water, and a pinch of salt. Let marinate for at least 10 minutes.
3. Soak the radishes in a bowl of ice-cold water until they crisp up and curl slightly.
4. In a medium bowl, combine the flour and baking powder. Sprinkle the shallots with a bit of water, then toss in the flour mixture until coated.
5. In a high-sided saucepan over medium heat, warm the oil to 350°F (175°C). Add the shallots and fry until golden brown. Remove with a slotted spoon and drain on paper towels. Sprinkle with salt.
6. In a small saucepan over medium-low heat, melt and brown the butter until it turns a nutty caramel color. Remove from heat, and let the browned solids settle to the bottom.
7. Peel the eggs and place them in the center of 4 plates.
8. Slice the potatoes and arrange them around the eggs. Add pieces of herring, marinated cucumber, and red onion to the plate.
9. Dollop with sour cream, and sprinkle with chives, microgreens, and dill. Top with the fried shallots and the radishes.
10. Drizzle plates with brown butter and grate horseradish over the top. Sprinkle with flaky salt and serve immediately.

burger with egg, avocado & sriracha mayo

Consider this—ground chuck patty, avocado, melted cheese, homemade Sriracha mayo, lime-marinated onions, an over-easy egg, and a bit of fresh cilantro—the ultimate burger.

Makes 4 burgers

½ cup (120 g) American-Style Whole-Egg Mayonnaise (page 39)
1 tablespoon Sriracha
1 white onion, finely sliced
1 tablespoon freshly squeezed lime juice
1 teaspoon granulated sugar
Salt
1 ⅓ pounds (600 g) freshly ground chuck
1 tablespoon olive oil
Freshly ground black pepper
4 Brioche Buns (page 61)
8 slices cheese, such as Edam, cheddar, or Gouda
4 tablespoons butter, divided
4 eggs
2 avocados, mashed
Leaves from 1 bunch cilantro

1. In a small bowl, combine the mayonnaise and Sriracha.
2. Preheat the oven to 300°F (150°C).
3. In a small bowl, combine the onion with lime juice, sugar, and a pinch of salt. Let marinate while you prepare the burgers.
4. Shape the ground meat into 4 equal patties. In a large skillet over medium to medium-high heat, warm the olive oil. Grill or cook in a hot pan for about 4 minutes on each side for medium-rare. Season with salt and pepper, and remove from pan.
5. Halve the brioche buns and place in the skillet, cut side down. Toast until golden. Line a baking sheet with parchment paper. Place the bottoms of the buns on the baking sheet and top each with 2 slices of cheese. Transfer to the oven until the cheese is melted.
6. Wipe out the skillet, and, one at a time, add 1 tablespoon of butter and fry the eggs over-easy, keeping the yolks runny (Classic French Fried Egg, page 14). Season with salt.
7. Place burgers on the bottom buns. Add the marinated onion, mashed avocado, sriracha mayo, cilantro, and fried egg. Serve immediately.

mains

With bright vegetables, herbs, and crispy marinated pork, this salad is reminiscent of *larb*, which is my absolute favorite Thai dish.

vietnamese salad with egg

Makes 4 servings

2 carrots

5 ½ ounces (150 g) daikon radish

2 limes, divided

2 tablespoons fish sauce

2 teaspoons granulated sugar

1 garlic clove, finely chopped, divided

1 ½ tablespoons finely chopped ginger, divided

1 red chili, such as Fresno or red jalapeño, seeded and finely chopped, divided

2 teaspoons sesame oil

4 tablespoons neutral oil, divided

7 ounces (200 g) ground pork

Salt

1 ½ tablespoons finely chopped Thai basil, plus ¼ cup (6 g) fresh leaves

1 ½ tablespoons finely chopped cilantro, plus ¼ cup (6 g) fresh leaves

1 ½ tablespoons finely chopped mint, plus ¼ cup (6 g) fresh leaves

6 eggs

1. Peel the carrots and daikon, slice thinly lengthwise, then cut into thin julienne strips. Prepare a bowl of ice water and submerge the carrot and daikon to keep them crisp until serving.

2. Juice 1 of the limes into a small bowl. Add the fish sauce and sugar. Add half the chopped garlic, ½ tablespoon of the ginger, and half the chili.

3. In a large skillet over medium-high heat, warm the sesame oil and 2 tablespoons of the neutral oil. Add the pork and the remaining garlic, ginger, and chili, and sauté until the meat is browned. Season to taste with salt, and stir in the chopped basil, cilantro, and mint. Transfer the pork to a plate, and wipe out the skillet.

4. In the skillet, use the remaining 2 tablespoons of oil to fry the eggs over easy (Classic French Fried Egg, page 14). Cook until the whites are set and the yolks are just firm enough to slice.

5. Slice the eggs into thin strips and season to taste with salt.

6. On a platter, layer the egg strips, basil, cilantro, and mint leaves, pork, carrot, and daikon. Drizzle with the dressing. Cut the remaining lime into wedges and serve alongside.

chicken egg soup with black rice

I finish this soup, inspired by Vietnamese phở, by cracking eggs directly into the broth to let them poach. The herbs are served on the side, allowing you to add as much as you like. Although not traditional, I swap black rice for the rice noodles to add heartiness.

Makes 4 servings

⅔ cup (135 g) black rice
1 tablespoon neutral oil
10 ½ ounces (300 g) boneless chicken thighs
Salt
2 yellow onions, sliced
2 garlic cloves, finely chopped
1 red chili, such as Fresno or red jalapeño, finely sliced
3 tablespoons fish sauce
2 star anise pods
1 teaspoon whole coriander seeds
2 cups fresh herbs (a combination of Thai basil, cilantro, and mint), divided
1 4-inch (10-cm) piece ginger, finely sliced
1 ¼ cups (125 g) fresh bean sprouts, divided
1 bunch radishes, trimmed and halved
4 eggs

1. Cook the rice according to package instructions.
2. In a large soup pot over medium-high heat, warm the oil and add the chicken. Cook, turning, until browned on both sides. Season with salt.
3. Add the onions, garlic, and chili to the pot. Sauté for 3 minutes.
4. Add 4 ¼ cups (1 l) water and the fish sauce, star anise, and coriander. Bring to a boil, then reduce heat to low and simmer, covered, for 1 hour.
5. Remove the chicken from the pot and shred. Return to the pot, and adjust seasoning as needed with salt and additional fish sauce.
6. Add ½ cup of the herbs, the ginger, ¾ cup (75 g) of the bean sprouts, the radishes, and the cooked rice to the pot. Gently crack the eggs into the soup and let them poach for about 5 minutes, until just set, covering the pot if necessary to help them cook.
7. Serve the soup with the remaining herbs and bean sprouts on the side.

bibimbap

Bibimbap, a Korean rice bowl, can take many forms. It can be made with beef, shredded chicken, crispy fried ground pork, seared salmon, or shrimp. The eggs vary too—sometimes they're boiled, sometimes fried, and sometimes raw yolks are used. But that's all part of the fun; this is a recipe to make all your own.

Makes 4 servings

- 1 ⅓ pounds (600 g) beef sirloin, sliced
- 2 garlic cloves, 1 finely grated and 1 chopped
- 6 teaspoons sesame oil, divided
- ½ cup (120 ml) Japanese soy sauce, plus more for serving
- 3 tablespoons rice vinegar, divided
- 1 ½ tablespoons granulated sugar
- 5 ½ ounces (150 g) fresh bean sprouts
- Salt
- 3 ½ ounces (100 g) daikon, finely julienned
- 3 ½ ounces (100 g) carrot, finely julienned
- 1 ⅔ cups (350 g) uncooked sushi rice
- 7 ounces (200 g) fresh spinach leaves
- 2 tablespoons neutral oil
- 1 English cucumber, thinly sliced
- 1 ¼ cups (150 g) kimchi
- 6 tablespoons gochujang (Korean chili paste)
- 4 63-degree eggs (Cooking a 63-Degree Egg, page 32)

1. In a large container, combine the beef with the grated garlic, 2 teaspoons sesame oil, soy sauce, 1 tablespoon rice vinegar, and the sugar. Let marinate for at least 30 minutes in the refrigerator.

2. In a large bowl, combine the bean sprouts with 1 ½ teaspoons sesame oil and ½ teaspoon salt. Let rest for at least 10 minutes.

3. In another large bowl, combine the daikon and carrot with 2 teaspoons sesame oil, 2 tablespoons rice vinegar, ⅛ teaspoon salt, and the chopped garlic. Let rest for at least 10 minutes.

4. Rinse the rice thoroughly under cold running water. Place in a pot with 2 ½ cups (600 ml) water and ½ teaspoon salt. Bring to a boil without a lid, then reduce the heat. Cover and simmer for about 20 minutes until the rice is tender. Remove from heat and let steam.

5. In a large skillet over medium heat, warm ½ teaspoon sesame oil and add the spinach. Sauté until wilted. Season with salt to taste and set aside on a plate. Wipe out the skillet.

6. Return the skillet to medium-high heat and add the neutral oil and then the marinated beef, cooking in batches if necessary. Cook until browned on all sides.

7. Divide the rice among 4 large bowls. Place the bean sprouts, daikon-carrot mixture, spinach, beef, cucumber, kimchi, and gochujang around the edges. Finish each bowl by placing 1 egg in the middle. Serve with soy sauce, if desired.

mains

bánh xèo

Bánh xèo is a delicious, crispy fried pancake served with *nước chấm*. This classic, all-purpose Vietnamese dipping sauce has a sweet, salty, funky flavor from the fish sauce and sugar, with a hint of tanginess from the lime.

Makes 4 pancakes

Batter

Generous ¾ cup (about 90 g) rice flour

1 ¼ cups (300 ml) coconut milk

1 teaspoon turmeric

Generous ¾ cup (about 200 ml) cold water

2 eggs

2 tablespoons fish sauce

Neutral oil, for frying

Nước Chấm

½ lemongrass stalk, smashed and finely chopped

2 tablespoons palm sugar or raw sugar

1 garlic clove, finely chopped

1–2 red chilies, such as Fresno or red jalapeño, seeded and finely chopped

3 tablespoons freshly squeezed lime juice

4 tablespoons fish sauce

2 tablespoons finely chopped cilantro

Filling

5 ½ ounces (150 g) fresh bean sprouts

¾ cup fresh herbs (a combination of Thai basil, cilantro, and mint)

7 ounces (200 g) small shrimp, cooked and peeled

Batter

1 In a medium bowl, combine the rice flour, coconut milk, and turmeric, and whisk until smooth. Whisk in the cold water, eggs, and fish sauce. Let the batter rest in the refrigerator for 30 minutes while you prepare the *nước chấm* and filling.

Nước chấm

2 To make the *nước chấm*, combine the lemongrass with ¼ cup (60 ml) water and the sugar in a small pot. Bring to a simmer and cook for 3 minutes. Strain, reserving the liquid and discarding the lemongrass, and, in a bowl, mix the liquid the garlic, chili, lime juice, fish sauce, and cilantro.

Crêpes

3 In a large skillet over medium heat, warm 1 tablespoon oil. When the pan is hot, pour in a ladleful of batter to cover the pan thinly. The batter should sizzle when it hits the pan.

4 Cook until crispy, then flip and cook the other side. Transfer to a plate and fill with bean sprouts, herbs, and shrimp. Repeat the process 3 more times. Drizzle each crêpe with *nước chấm* and serve.

egg ramen noodles

Making your own egg noodles for ramen is similar to the technique used for Egg Pasta (page 139). Here, a small amount of cornstarch combines with the flour to give the noodles a nice texture that allows broth to cling to them in a ramen bowl. The dough is kneaded thoroughly to achieve a chewy consistency that holds up in hot broth. You can either roll out the dough thinly, fold it, and cut it into long noodles or use a pasta machine.

Makes 4–6 servings

2 ½ cups (300 g) 00 flour
1 tablespoon cornstarch, plus more for dusting
4 eggs
Salt

Special equipment: deep-fry thermometer

1. In a large bowl, combine the flour, cornstarch, and eggs and mix with a wooden spoon or your hands. The dough should be firm.
2. Turn the dough out onto a clean surface and knead by hand for about 10 minutes, until smooth and elastic. Wrap in plastic wrap and let rest at room temperature for 1 hour.
3. Divide the dough into 6 pieces. Flatten each piece and dust with cornstarch.
4. Use a pasta machine to roll out the dough to a thickness of about 2 mm, dusting with cornstarch as you work to prevent sticking. Cut dough sheets into the thinnest-width noodles your machine can make.
5. Boil in salted water for about 1 ½ minutes. Transfer directly into broth when ready to serve.

mains

ramen broth

Cooking a truly great Japanese ramen broth requires skill—or rather, making the broth itself is simple, but balancing the flavors, fat, and toppings is an art.

I make a very basic broth using just water, chicken, and salt. The bird should be of high quality, with a good layer of fat on its skin. Gently simmering a whole chicken (not broken into pieces as is customary) produces a clean, light broth that reflects Japanese minimalism. This is the base recipe. When you later prepare your ramen, the broth is combined with your choice of tare (seasoning) to achieve the unique flavor, depth, and character you're looking for.

Makes 5 ¼ quarts (5 l)

1 whole chicken or hen
  3-4 pounds (1 ⅓-1 ¾ kg)
Salt

1. Place the whole chicken in a large pot.
2. Add water to cover the chicken about 5 ¾ quarts (5 ½ l) and bring to a gentle boil. Skim off any foam that rises to the surface.
3. Cover the pot, and simmer for 1 ½-2 hours.
4. Remove the chicken from the broth and set aside. (Once cool enough to handle, pull the meat from the chicken and reserve for other uses, like adding to ramen dishes.)
5. Strain the broth into a large container and season with salt to taste. (Use a light hand with the salt, as you will be adding other seasonings later when you make ramen.) Store in the refrigerator for up to 5 days.

soy-pickled eggs

Makes 6

½ cup (120 ml) Japanese soy sauce
¼ cup (60 ml) mirin
1 tablespoon coarsely chopped ginger
6 boiled 5-minute eggs (pages 9-10), cooled

1. In a small saucepan over medium heat, combine the soy sauce, mirin, ½ cup (120 ml) water, and ginger. Bring to a simmer and cook for 5 minutes.
2. Let the mixture cool slightly, then pour into a heatproof container with a lid. Peel the eggs and place them in the marinade.
3. Refrigerate, covered, for at least 10 hours or up to 1 day. Halve the eggs and serve with ramen or rice dishes.

kimchi ramen with 64-degree egg

With its many textures and layered flavors, ramen is as close to a perfect food as one can get. And this one is all about the toppings. The recipe calls for nearly a ½ cup of kimchi per serving, but add as much or as little as you wish.

Makes 4 servings

3 tablespoons neutral oil, divided
16 Padrón or shishito peppers
2 ears of corn, kernels cut from cobs
Salt
1 pound (500 g) ground pork
1 ½ tablespoons fish sauce
1 teaspoon sesame oil
1 recipe Egg Ramen Noodles (page 161)
1 recipe Ramen Broth (page 162)
4 tablespoons gochujang (Korean chili paste), divided
6 tablespoons Japanese soy sauce, divided
6 scallions, thinly sliced (reserve a few for garnish)
1 ⅔ cups (250 g) kimchi
Leaves and tender stems from 2 bunches cilantro
4–6 boiled 64-degree eggs (page 32)
½ cup (75 g) finely chopped peanuts, for garnish

1. In a large skillet over high heat, warm 1 tablespoon of the oil. Add the peppers and sauté, turning once, for about 5 minutes or until blistered. Transfer peppers to a plate.

2. In the skillet over medium heat, warm 1 more tablespoon of oil and add the corn kernels and a pinch of salt. Sauté 2 minutes, until slightly softened. Transfer corn to a bowl.

3. In the skillet over medium-high heat, warm the remaining 1 tablespoon of oil and add the ground pork, fish sauce, and sesame oil. Sauté until meat is well-browned.

4. Bring a pot of salted water to a boil and add the noodles; cook for 1 ½ minutes, then drain. In a large pot, bring the ramen broth to a simmer.

5. Divide the broth between 4 large serving bowls. To each bowl, stir in 1 tablespoon gochujang and 1 ½ tablespoons soy sauce.

6. Divide the noodles between the bowls and top with pork, scallions, peppers, corn, kimchi, cilantro, and eggs. Sprinkle with peanuts and extra scallions.

miso & sesame ramen

The salty miso and sesame in this hearty ramen will warm you right up on cold days. Drizzle with chili oil to taste—I usually add a lot.

Makes 4 servings

4 portions Chashu Pork (right)

1 ½ quarts (1 ½ l) Ramen Broth (page 162)

Salt

2 small heads bok choy, halved

4 portions Egg Ramen Noodles (page 161)

3 tablespoons shiro miso (white miso), divided

3 tablespoons tahini, divided

4 Soy-Pickled Eggs (page 162), prepared 1 day before serving

2 scallions, finely sliced

4 tablespoons Crunchy Chili Oil (page 75)

2 tablespoons sesame seeds, toasted and crushed or ground

Special equipment: cooking blowtorch (optional)

1. Slice the chashu pork into 8 pieces and use a blowtorch or your oven's broiler to caramelize the surface, rendering some of the fat.
2. In a large pot, bring the broth to a simmer.
3. Bring a separate large pot of salted water to a boil.
4. Add the bok choy and blanch for 1 minute, then remove with a slotted spoon and set aside. Add the noodles and cook for 1 ½ minutes, then drain.
5. Divide miso and tahini between 4 serving bowls. Pour in a little broth to each bowl and whisk in the miso and tahini.
6. Divide noodles between the bowls, then fill each bowl with more broth.
7. Top each bowl with eggs, bok choy, scallions, chashu pork, chili oil, and sesame seeds.

chashu pork

Makes 6 servings

1 cup (240 ml) Japanese soy sauce
¾ cup (180 ml) mirin
3 scallions, trimmed
1 4-inch (10-cm) piece ginger, sliced
3 garlic cloves, peeled and crushed
2 ¾ pounds (1 ¼ kg) pork belly, skin on

1. Preheat the oven to 300°F (150°C).
2. In a deep baking dish or ovenproof pot, combine ¾ cup (180 ml) water with the soy sauce, mirin, scallions, ginger, and garlic.
3. Place the pork belly in the liquid, skin side down.
4. Cover with a lid or aluminum foil and place on the lower rack of the oven. Reduce the heat to 250°F (125°C).
5. Bake for 4 hours, flipping the pork halfway through so that both sides have a chance to soak in the marinade.
6. Remove the pork from the oven and let it cool in the liquid. Cover with plastic wrap and refrigerate overnight.
7. When ready to serve, slice the pork thinly and reheat it in the oven under the broiler, or use a blowtorch to caramelize the surface.

shio tofu ramen

If you want to make this ramen completely vegetarian, simply replace the chicken broth with vegetable or mushroom broth.

Makes 4 servings

1 ½ quarts (1 ½ l) Ramen Broth (page 162)
Salt
4 portions Egg Ramen Noodles (page 161)
4 Soy-Pickled Eggs (page 162)
14 ounces (400 g) silken tofu, diced
5 ounces (150 g) fresh bean sprouts
3 scallions, finely sliced
1 sheet nori, cut into 4 pieces

1. In a large pot, bring the broth to a simmer. Season to taste with salt.
2. Bring a separate large pot of salted water to a boil. Add the noodles and cook for 1 ½ minutes, then drain.
3. Divide the broth between 4 serving bowls. Add noodles to each bowl, then top with eggs, tofu, bean sprouts, and scallions.
4. Garnish each bowl with a piece of nori. Serve immediately.

miso & sesame ramen, soy-pickled eggs, and shio tofu ramen

kimchi udon & egg

Imagine a creamy carbonara where the egg pasta is swapped out for thick, springy udon noodles and mixed with bacon, kimchi, and egg yolk to create a decadent crowd-pleaser. When *Bon Appétit* featured a similar recipe a few years ago, it became one of the most searched recipes on the magazine's website. I usually buy udon noodles that come vacuum-packed, as I find them superior to the dried version.

Makes 4 servings

5 ounces (140 g) bacon

Salt

14 ounces (400 g) udon noodles

½ cup (120 ml) juice from a jar of kimchi, plus 1 ¼ cups (188 g) kimchi, roughly chopped

3 ½ ounces (100 g) butter

4 egg yolks

4 scallions, finely sliced

2 tablespoons toasted sesame seeds (preferably a mix of black and white)

1. In a medium deep-sided skillet over medium-high heat, cook the bacon until crispy. Drain on paper towels, then chop roughly and set aside.

2. Bring a large pot of salted water to a boil and cook udon according to package instructions. Drain and set aside.

3. In a large skillet over medium heat, combine the kimchi juice and butter. Once butter is melted, stir in the noodles, kimchi, and bacon.

4. Serve in bowls topped with an egg yolk, scallions, and sesame seeds.

"son-in-law" thai eggs

Traditionally, this Thai dish is made with hard-boiled eggs because, as the joke goes in Thailand, it's the only thing a son-in-law can manage to cook. However, I have a bit more faith in men and make the dish with fried eggs, then drizzle the delicious dressing made of fish sauce, tamarind, lime, and chilies over the top.

Makes 4 servings

½ lemongrass stalk, finely sliced
2 shallots, finely sliced
2 tablespoons fish sauce
2 tablespoons tamarind sauce
2 tablespoons freshly squeezed lime juice
1 tablespoon granulated sugar
1–3 small Thai chilies or 1 red chili pepper, seeded and thinly sliced
2 tablespoons roasted peanuts
1 quart (1 l) neutral oil, for frying
8 eggs
½ cup (8 g) fresh cilantro sprigs
Cooked jasmine or sticky rice, for serving

Special equipment: deep-fry thermometer

1. In a medium bowl, combine the lemongrass, shallots, fish sauce, 2 tablespoons water, tamarind sauce, lime juice, sugar, chilies, and peanuts.
2. In a pot or deep pan, heat the oil to 350°F (175°C).
3. Crack the eggs into a bowl, then slide them gently into the hot oil. Only add a few at a time to avoid crowding.
4. Fry eggs for about 1 minute, until crispy. Remove from the oil with a heatproof slotted spoon or spider (skimmer), and drain on paper towels. Repeat until all eggs are cooked.
5. Arrange the eggs on a platter and top with cilantro. Drizzle the dressing over the eggs.
6. Serve with rice.

oto

Sweet potatoes and red onions with a soft-boiled egg may sound simple, but this straightforward dish deserves some attention. In Ghana, Oto is a staple at weddings, birthdays, and other celebrations. The traditional recipe uses yams, but I've swapped them for sweet potatoes since they're easier to find. If you happen to come across yams or cassava, feel free to use those instead.

In this dish, the focus should be on the red onions, cooked slowly in butter or oil until they become sweet and full of flavor. Enjoy the dish as it is, or serve it with fish or chicken.

Makes 4 servings

Salt
1 ¾ pounds (800 g) sweet potatoes, peeled and chopped
7 tablespoons (100 g) butter
3 red onions, finely chopped
3 boiled 6-minute eggs (pages 9-10)

1. Bring a large pot of salted water to a boil. Add the potatoes and cook until tender. Drain and set aside.
2. In a large skillet over low heat, melt the butter and sauté onions for about 10 minutes until soft and light brown.
3. In a large bowl, mash the sweet potatoes. Mix in the onions and season with salt to taste. Transfer to a serving plate.
4. Peel and halve the soft-boiled eggs, then place on top of the sweet potatoes, and serve.

chawanmushi

tsukune

oyakodon

In this dish, the definition of Japanese comfort food, a delicious dashi broth with chicken is poured over freshly cooked rice and drizzled with beaten egg. Dashi can be purchased at international grocery stores in liquid form or in a powder you mix with water. You can also substitute a miso broth for the dashi for a slightly more complex flavor.

Makes 4 servings

2 cups (500 g) short-grain sushi rice, uncooked • 1 ⅔ cups (400 ml) prepared dashi broth • 2 tablespoons soy sauce • 1 ½ tablespoons mirin • 10 ½ ounces (300 g) boneless skinless chicken thigh, sliced • 1 yellow onion, finely sliced • 3 eggs, beaten • 1 ½ tablespoons rice vinegar • 2 scallions, finely sliced • 1 tablespoon toasted sesame seeds

1. Cook the rice according to package instructions.
2. In a large, high-sided skillet over medium heat, warm the dashi.
3. Add the soy sauce, mirin, and chicken. Simmer over low heat for about 10 minutes, until chicken is cooked through.
4. Add the onion and drizzle the eggs over the broth.
5. Allow the eggs to set like an omelet in the broth.
6. Divide the rice between 4 bowls, or serve in 1 large bowl. Drizzle the vinegar over the rice, then ladle the chicken, eggs, and broth over the rice. The broth will soak into the hot rice.
7. Garnish with scallions and sesame seeds. Serve immediately.

chawan-mushi

Chawanmushi is a Japanese steamed egg custard—think of it as a savory crème brûlée traditionally flavored with dashi, though I like to use miso. I often serve it drizzled with a little browned butter as a starter or alongside other small dishes.

Makes 4 servings

1 ½ tablespoons shiro miso (white miso) • 1 teaspoon granulated sugar • 2 teaspoons Japanese soy sauce • 3 eggs, beaten • 7 tablespoons (100 g) butter

Special equipment: 4 small ramekins, bamboo steamer or other steamer that can hold the ramekins

1. In a medium saucepan over medium-low heat, combine the miso, sugar, soy sauce, and ⅔ cup (160 ml) water. Whisk until miso is dissolved, and then let cool.
2. Stir in the eggs until well combined.
3. Divide the mixture between the 4 ramekins. Remove any bubbles on the surface by pressing a paper towel to the surface to absorb them.
4. Cover the ramekins with plastic wrap. Prepare the steamer setup, and then add the ramekins and steam for 8–10 minutes.
5. While the custards steam, in a small saucepan over medium heat, melt and brown the butter until it smells nutty and caramel-like.
6. Top steamed custards with browned butter and serve immediately.

tsukune

In Japan, a favorite izakaya snack is freshly grilled chicken skewers dipped in creamy egg yolk. When replicating the dish at home, follow this simple rule for perfect skewers: don't take shortcuts by using pre-ground chicken. The chicken should be hand-chopped to keep the skewers moist and flavorful.

Makes 4 servings

12 ½ ounces (350 g) boneless skinless chicken thighs, trimmed of fat • 1 ½ tablespoons shiro miso (white miso) • 2 scallions, finely sliced • 2 tablespoons plus 2 teaspoons Japanese soy sauce, divided • 6 large shiso leaves, finely sliced (optional) • Sesame oil, for shaping • 1 tablespoon mirin • 4 egg yolks, for serving

Special equipment: wooden skewers

1. Place 8 wooden skewers in a high-sided dish or baking pan and pour in enough water to cover. Let soak for at least 30 minutes while you prepare the chicken.
2. Using a sharp knife, finely mince the chicken.
3. In a medium bowl, combine the chicken with the miso, scallions, 2 tablespoons soy sauce, and the shiso leaves, if using. Stir the mixture until smooth.
4. Divide the chicken mixture into 8 equal portions. Oil your hands with sesame oil and shape the chicken into round balls. Mold each ball around 1 skewer into an oval patty shape.
5. In a small bowl, combine the remaining 2 teaspoons soy sauce and the mirin. Grill or pan-fry the skewers for about 10 minutes, until browned and cooked through. Toward the end of the cooking time, brush the chicken with the soy sauce and mirin to create a savory glaze.
6. Serve 2 skewers per person, with an egg yolk on the side for dipping.

Tip: Some variations of the tsukune recipe suggest stirring a small amount of soy, mirin, or dashi into the egg yolk to create an enhanced sauce for dipping the skewers.

tamago kake gohan

Consider this the rice version of pasta carbonara. The eggs are stirred into steaming-hot rice, creating a sticky, creamy sauce that coats each grain. The traditional version is topped with nori and sesame seeds, but I like the Japanese seasoning furikake and chives.

Makes 4 servings

2 cups (500 g) short-grain sushi rice, uncooked • 4 small eggs plus 4 egg yolks, divided • 1 tablespoon Japanese soy sauce • 4 teaspoons mirin • 4 teaspoons rice vinegar • 2 tablespoons furikake • ½ tablespoon finely chopped chives

1. Cook the rice according to package instructions. Transfer the hot rice to a large bowl and crack in the whole eggs. Mix thoroughly to coat the rice evenly; the heat from the rice will lightly cook the eggs.
2. Add the soy sauce, mirin, and rice vinegar and mix into the rice.
3. Divide the rice between serving bowls. Make a small well in the rice and place an egg yolk in each.
4. Top with furikake and chives, and serve immediately.

torta pasqualina

This Italian Easter torte with a flaky phyllo crust has a stunning presentation thanks to the whole eggs baked inside. Traditionally, it is made with 33 layers of phyllo, representing the years of Jesus's life.

Makes 10 slices

- 7 tablespoons (100 g) butter, melted
- 1 (16-ounce/450-g) package phyllo dough, thawed if necessary
- 2 slices white sourdough bread, chopped or crumbled
- 17 ½ ounces (500 g) ricotta cheese
- 8 eggs, divided
- 1 ¾ ounces (50 g) finely grated Parmesan cheese
- 1 teaspoon dried oregano
- ⅛ teaspoon freshly grated nutmeg
- 17 ½ ounces (500 g) frozen spinach, thawed and squeezed dry
- Salt and freshly ground black pepper

Special equipment: 9 ½-inch (24-cm) round springform pan

1. Preheat the oven to 425°F (225°C).
2. Place the springform pan on a baking sheet, then brush the bottom and sides of the pan with melted butter. Next line the pan with phyllo dough sheets, brushing each sheet with melted butter as you place it. Overlap the sheets to create a crust on the bottom and sides of the pan, saving 5 sheets for the top of the torte.
3. In a large bowl, combine the bread, ricotta, 2 of the eggs, the Parmesan, oregano, nutmeg, and spinach. Season to taste with salt and pepper.
4. Fill the phyllo crust with the ricotta mixture. Make 6 wells in the filling and crack 6 eggs into the wells.
5. Cover with the remaining 5 sheets of phyllo dough, again brushing each sheet with melted butter.
6. Fold any overhanging phyllo dough down around the filling.
7. Place the baking sheet and pan in the center of the oven and bake for 1 hour or until the torte is golden brown.
8. Allow to cool slightly and slice. Serve warm or at room temperature.

pizza with eggs

A pizza topped with a runny egg is a thing of genius—and it can be eaten for breakfast, brunch, or dinner. But first, you need to perfect the crust. For the best results, let the dough cold ferment and bake it the next day using a pizza stone. The goal is to get the oven as hot as possible so the dough quickly becomes crisp and bubbles up with the toppings. If you don't have a pizza stone, preheat a baking sheet in the oven, then transfer the uncooked pizza onto the hot sheet. This "shocks" the dough and makes it crispy.

pizza dough

Makes four 10-12 inch (25-30 cm) pizzas

1 teaspoon dry active yeast
1 ¾ cups (420 ml) warm water
3 ⅓ cups (400 g) all-purpose flour + more for rolling
1 teaspoon salt
1 tablespoon olive oil

1. In a large bowl, combine the yeast and warm water. Let sit until foamy, about 5 minutes.
2. Stir in the flour and knead with a wooden spoon or your hands to form a smooth dough. When the dough is starting to come together, add the salt and knead to distribute.
3. Grease a large bowl with the olive oil. Place the dough in the bowl and cover with plastic wrap. Let rise overnight at room temperature.
4. Transfer the dough onto a floured surface. Divide into 4 or 8 equal pieces and roll gently into balls. At this point, all balls may be shaped into pizzas, or some may be frozen for later use.

pizza with chorizo & spinach

pizza bianca with pancetta & radicchio

pizza bianca with pancetta & radicchio

Makes two 10-12 inch (25-30 cm) pizzas

½ recipe Pizza Dough (page 182)

Scant ½ cup (100 g) crème fraîche

1 yellow onion, sliced

Zest of ½ lemon

½ teaspoon thyme leaves

2 ounces (55 g) radicchio, shredded

4 ½ ounces (125 g) buffalo mozzarella, torn into pieces

Scant ½ cup (50 g) grated Comté or Gruyère cheese

¼ cup (28 g) finely grated Parmesan cheese, plus more for garnish

3 ½ ounces (100 g) sliced pancetta

1-2 eggs

Flaky sea salt and freshly ground black pepper

Special equipment: pizza stone or baking sheet, pizza peel or cutting board

1. Place a pizza stone or baking sheet in the oven.
2. Preheat the oven to 525°F (275°C).
3. Roll out the pizza dough into 2 rounds and spread with crème fraîche.
4. Sprinkle with onion, lemon zest, and thyme.
5. Spread the radicchio on the pizza and top with mozzarella, Comté, and Parmesan. Layer the pancetta on top.
6. Create a space in the middle of the pizza and crack the egg(s) on top.
7. Use a pizza peel or cutting board to transfer the pizza to the baking sheet or stone.
8. Bake in the center of the oven for about 8 minutes, until the egg white is just set and the yolk remains creamy.
9. Top with additional Parmesan. Season to taste with salt and pepper.

pizza with chorizo & spinach

Makes two 10-12 inch (25-30 cm) pizzas

2 tablespoons olive oil
½ garlic clove, finely grated
1 ½ tablespoons tomato paste
½ can (7 ½ ounces/213 g) crushed tomatoes
Flaky sea salt and freshly ground black pepper
7 ounces (200 g) fresh baby spinach
½ recipe Pizza Dough (page 182)
4 ½ ounces (125 g) buffalo mozzarella, torn into pieces
4 ¼ ounces (120 g) dried chorizo, sliced
Scant 1 cup (100 g) grated Gouda or Edam
1-2 eggs

Special equipment: pizza stone or baking sheet, pizza peel or cutting board

1. In a skillet over medium-low heat, warm the oil and add the garlic and tomato paste. Fry, stirring, for 1 minute.
2. Add the crushed tomatoes and let simmer for 10 minutes. Season with salt and pepper to taste, and let cool.
3. Place a pizza stone or baking sheet in the oven.
4. Preheat the oven to 525°F (275°C).
5. In a separate small skillet over low heat, sauté the spinach with a little water until wilted. Set aside.
6. Roll out the pizza dough into 2 rounds, and spread with the tomato sauce.
7. Scatter pieces of mozzarella over the sauce, and top the mozzarella with chorizo and spinach. Finish by sprinkling with the grated cheese.
8. Create a space in the middle of the pizza and crack the egg(s) on top.
9. Use a pizza peel or cutting board to transfer the pizza to the baking sheet or stone.
10. Bake in the center of the oven for about 8 minutes, until the egg white is just set, but the yolk remains creamy.
11. Season to taste with salt and pepper.

Sweets & Cocktails

It's no surprise that eggs, with their richness and body, figure heavily in dessert. Those qualities add similar oomph to cocktails as well.

sweets & cocktails

pastéis de nata

The *pastéis de nata* is Portugal's claim to pastry fame—and one of the world's best sweet treats. These mini tarts are filled with vanilla custard and baked in the oven until golden brown, yielding a rich caramelized flavor.

Makes 12 mini tarts

Dough

1 ¼ cups (300 ml) whole milk, warmed to 100°F–115°F (38°C–46°C)

2 ½ teaspoons active dry yeast

¼ cup (50 g) granulated sugar

1 egg

½ teaspoon salt

3–3 ⅓ cups (360–425 g) all-purpose flour

21 tablespoons (300 g) very cold butter

Filling

1 cup (240 ml) whole milk, divided

1 cup (200 g) granulated sugar

Salt

Peel of 1 lemon, cut into thick strips

2 cinnamon sticks

¼ cup (30 g) all-purpose flour

8 egg yolks

Butter, for greasing muffin tins

Special equipment: cheese slicer, standard size muffin tin

Dough

1. In a large bowl, combine the warmed milk and the yeast. Allow the yeast to bloom for about 5 minutes. Stir in the sugar, egg, and salt. Whisk until smooth.

2. Add the flour, starting with 3 cups (360 g) and knead until a smooth dough forms. Add more flour if needed. Sprinkle the dough with a little flour, cover the bowl with plastic wrap, and let rise for 30 minutes at room temperature. Refrigerate for another 30 minutes, then roll out the dough to a 12 x 16-inch (30 x 40-cm) rectangle.

3. Use the cheese slicer to shave the butter over one half of the dough, leaving a ¾-inch (2-cm) border without butter. Fold the unbuttered half over the buttered half. Pinch the edges to seal in the butter.

4. Roll the dough to about ½ inch (1 cm) thick, then fold it into thirds like you're folding an envelope. Turn the dough 90 degrees and then repeat the rolling and folding.

5. Wrap the dough in plastic and chill for 30 minutes. Repeat rolling, folding, and chilling 4 more times. On the last round, roll the dough into a log about 2 inches (5 cm) in diameter, and cut in half horizontally. Wrap both halves in plastic wrap; place 1 in the refrigerator and chill for 1 hour; place the other in the freezer for later use.

Filling

6. In a medium saucepan, combine ¾ cup (180 ml) of the milk with 1 cup (240 ml) water. Add the sugar, a pinch of salt, lemon peel, and cinnamon sticks. Bring to a boil, then remove from heat and remove the lemon peel and cinnamon sticks.

7. In a medium bowl, whisk together the remaining ¼ cup (60 ml) milk and the flour. Stir into the milk-sugar mixture. Return to low heat and stir until the mixture thickens.

8. Transfer to a clean bowl and let cool slightly, then whisk in the egg yolks. Let cool completely.

Tarts

9. Preheat the oven to 450°F (230°C). Grease the muffin tin with butter and place on
10. a baking sheet.
11. Remove the dough log from the refrigerator, unwrap, and slice into rounds about ⅔ inch (1 ½ cm) thick. Press each round into a cup of the muffin tin, using your fingers to make sure the dough is evenly distributed on the bottom and up the sides.
12. Fill the tart shells with custard mixture, leaving a little space at the top. Bake in the center of the oven for about 10 minutes, until the pastry is golden and the filling is starting to brown in places.
13. Let tarts cool in the muffin tin before removing and transferring to a wire rack. Eat within 1 day, or store in an airtight container in the refrigerator for up to 3 days.

sweets & cocktails

custard pie

The key to this recipe is baking the pie for just the right amount of time. Too little and it will be runny; too much and it will resemble an omelet in both taste and texture. If you're an experienced crème brûlée cook, think of this filling as similar; the pie should have a slight jiggle when you remove it from the oven.

Makes 8–10 slices

Crust

½ cup (60 g) powdered sugar

1 ¼ cups (155 g) all-purpose flour, plus more for rolling

9 tablespoons (125 g) cold butter, cubed

1 teaspoon white wine vinegar

1 egg yolk

1 egg white, for brushing crust

Filling

3 eggs

¾ cup (150 g) granulated sugar

Scraped seeds from ½ vanilla bean

Salt

3 cups (720 ml) whole milk

½ teaspoon freshly grated nutmeg, divided

Whipped cream, for serving

Special equipment: 9 ½-inch (24-cm) round pie dish, pie weights or dried beans

Crust

1. In a large bowl, combine the powdered sugar and flour. Using a pastry cutter or two forks, cut in the butter, vinegar, and egg yolk until crumbly (small lumps of butter will remain). Shape into a ball, flatten, wrap in plastic wrap, and refrigerate for at least 30 minutes.

2. On a floured surface, roll out the dough to about ⅛ inch (3 mm) thick. Transfer the dough to the pie dish and press into place, trimming any excess.

3. Prick the bottom of the dough with a fork. Transfer the pie dish to the freezer and freeze for 30 minutes.

4. Preheat the oven to 400°F (200°C).

5. Blind bake the crust: Place a piece of parchment paper over the dough and then top with the pie weights or dried beans, pressing them gently into the corners. Bake for about 10 minutes. Carefully remove parchment and pie weights from the crust.

6. Brush the crust with egg white and return to the oven to bake for 3 more minutes. Let cool.

Filling

7. In a large bowl, beat the eggs. Whisk in the sugar, vanilla seeds, a pinch of salt, milk, and half the nutmeg.

8. Fill the pie crust with the mixture and bake in the center of the oven for about 45 minutes, until just set but slightly wobbly.

9. Remove from the oven and grate the remaining nutmeg over the top. Let cool, and then refrigerate for at least 3 hours or up to overnight before serving. Slice and serve with a dollop of whipped cream.

dan tat

With a shortcrust pastry base and a slightly firmer custard filling than its Portuguese counterpart, *dan tat* is one of the most famous Chinese pastries. Unlike *pastéis de nata* (page 188), these egg tarts should have little to no color on the surface, a finish achieved by baking them in a cooler oven.

Makes about 12 tarts

Dough
10 ½ tablespoons cold butter, plus more for greasing
1 ⅔ cups (210 g) all-purpose flour
3 ⅓ cups (400 g) powdered sugar
1 egg
¼ teaspoon salt

Filling
⅔ cup (135 g) granulated sugar
2 teaspoons cornstarch
⅛ teaspoon salt
¾ cup (180 ml) whole milk
⅔ cup (160 ml) heavy cream
7 egg yolks

Special equipment: stand mixer fitted with the paddle attachment, standard size muffin tin or 12 small tart molds

1. Preheat the oven to 325°F (165° C) with a rack in the lowest position.
2. Grease a muffin tin or 12 tart molds with butter and place on a baking sheet.
3. Make the dough: In the stand mixer, combine the butter, flour, and powdered sugar and mix on medium speed to form a crumbly dough. Add the egg and salt, mixing only enough to form a cohesive dough. Shape dough into a log and slice into 12 equal pieces.
4. Press each piece into a cup of the muffin tins or tart molds, using your fingers to make sure the dough is evenly distributed on the bottom and up the sides. Chill in the refrigerator for at least 30 minutes.
5. While the dough chills, make the filling: in a large bowl, combine the sugar, cornstarch, and salt. Whisk in the milk, cream, and egg yolks until smooth.
6. Fill the chilled dough with the filling, leaving a little space at the top.
7. Bake for about 20-22 minutes, covering loosely with foil if the tops begin to brown. The filling should set but still be slightly jiggly.
8. Let tarts cool in the muffin tin or molds before removing and transferring to a wire rack. Eat within 1 day, or store in an airtight container in the refrigerator for up to 3 days.

the notorious soufflé

Attempting to whip up soufflé batter and then getting it to rise in the oven is a daunting task. But don't worry; there are a few tricks to mastering it.

Never overbake a soufflé. The art is in getting the batter to rise out of the dish while still keeping a creamy center. If overbaked, the structure will collapse when it comes out of the oven. However, if a small portion of the center remains undercooked, the dessert will hold its shape nicely until served and will only collapse when you dip a spoon into its fluffy mass.

While stylish cups, polka-dotted bowls, or designer square porcelain dishes may look appealing, for best results, go with a classic, straight-sided French soufflé dish, also known as a cocotte. It is specifically crafted to ensure the batter bakes perfectly.

There are two ways to shape a soufflé. The first is to pipe a neat dollop into the dish, allowing it to rise beautifully and form a round peak in the oven. The second is to pipe a generous amount into the dish, then use a palette knife to level the top so it aligns with the edges of the dish. This creates a flat-topped soufflé. There's no noticeable difference in baking between the two methods, but the peaked version can sometimes develop a more baked top since it stands higher in the oven.

berry soufflé

Makes 6 servings

1 ½ cups (225 g) berries, such as blueberries, raspberries, blackberries, or cloudberries

¾ cup (150 g) granulated sugar, divided, plus more for ramekins

2 tablespoons cornstarch

1 ½ tablespoons cold water

Butter, for greasing

4 egg whites

Special equipment:
6 (5-6-ounce/150-180-ml) ramekins, immersion blender, stand mixer fitted with the whisk attachment, piping bag

1. In a medium saucepan over medium-low heat, cook the berries and half the sugar. Use the immersion blender to blend the berries into a purée, then strain out the seeds through a fine-mesh sieve. Return the purée to the saucepan.

2. In a small bowl, combine the cornstarch and water to make a slurry, then stir it into the berry purée. Cook over medium heat, stirring, until the mixture thickens. Transfer to a large bowl and cool to room temperature.

3. Preheat the oven to 350°F (175°C). Grease the ramekins with butter and dust with sugar, then place on a baking sheet.

4. To the bowl of the stand mixer, add the egg whites. Whip on medium-high speed until foamy, and then gradually add the remaining sugar, whipping until stiff peaks form.

5. Mix a scant ½ cup of the meringue into the berry mixture to lighten it, then gently fold in the remaining meringue.

6. Fill a piping bag with the mixture.

7. Pipe the soufflé mixture into the ramekins. Smooth the tops and then gently run your fingertip around the edge of the ramekins (so the batter loosens and rises properly in the oven). Bake on the lower rack of the oven for 8–10 minutes, until soufflés are browned, puffed, and still slightly wobbly. Serve immediately.

apple & nut soufflé

Makes 6 servings

⅔ cup (80 g) hazelnuts

7 ounces (200 g) tart apples, peeled and diced

⅔ cup (260 g) granulated sugar, divided

1 ½ tablespoons cornstarch

Butter, for greasing

⅔ cup (130 g) raw sugar

4 egg whites

Special equipment: food processor, immersion blender, 6 (5–6-ounce/150–180-ml) ramekins, stand mixer fitted with the whisk attachment, piping bag

1. Preheat the oven to 350°F (175°C). Place the hazelnuts on a baking sheet and toast in the oven for about 10 minutes, until fragrant and skins are slightly blackened. Remove from the oven and transfer the nuts to a clean kitchen towel. Enclose the nuts in the towel, and rub off the skins.
2. Transfer the nuts to the food processor and process into a smooth paste.
3. In a medium saucepan over medium heat, combine the apples, a scant ½ cup of the granulated sugar, and ½ cup (120 ml) water, and stir until soft. Using the immersion blender, blend into a smooth purée.
4. In a small bowl, combine the cornstarch and 2 tablespoons water to make a slurry. Stir into the apple purée, and cook until the mixture thickens. Transfer to a large bowl.
5. Stir the hazelnut paste into the apple mixture, and let cool to room temperature.
6. Preheat the oven to 350°F (175°C) once again or leave the oven on after toasting the hazelnuts. Grease the ramekins with butter and dust with the raw sugar, then place on a baking sheet.
7. To the bowl of the stand mixer, add the egg whites. Whip on medium-high speed until foamy, then gradually add the remaining granulated sugar, whipping until stiff peaks form.
8. Mix a scant ½ cup of the meringue into the apple-nut mixture to lighten it, then gently fold in the remaining meringue.
9. Fill a piping bag with the mixture.
10. Pipe the soufflé mixture into the ramekins. Smooth the tops and then gently run your fingertip around the edge of the ramekins (so the batter loosens and rises properly in the oven). Bake on the lower rack of the oven for 8–10 minutes, until soufflés are browned, puffed, and still slightly wobbly. Serve immediately.

sweets & cocktails

chocolate soufflé with sea salt

Makes 6 servings

¾ cup (180 ml) heavy cream

6 ⅓ ounces (180 g) dark chocolate (70%), finely chopped

4 eggs

1 ½ tablespoons cornstarch

Butter, for greasing

Scant ½ cup (about 190 g) granulated sugar, plus more for the ramekins

½ teaspoon flaky sea salt

Special equipment: 6 (5–6-ounce/150–180-ml) ramekins, stand mixer fitted with the whisk attachment, piping bag

1. In a large saucepan over medium heat, warm the cream until bubbles appear. Remove from heat, and stir in the chocolate, whisking until it melts and the mixture is smooth. Let cool.

2. Separate the eggs into yolks and whites. Mix the yolks into the chocolate mixture until smooth. Sift in the cornstarch and mix well. Transfer chocolate mixture to a large bowl.

3. Preheat the oven to 350°F (175°C). Grease the ramekins with butter and dust with sugar, then place on a baking sheet.

4. To the bowl of the stand mixer, add the egg whites. Whip on medium-high speed until foamy, then gradually add the scant ½ cup sugar, whipping until stiff peaks form.

5. Mix ⅓ cup of the meringue into the chocolate mixture to lighten it, then gently fold in the remaining meringue. Add the salt and fold gently to combine.

6. Fill a piping bag with the mixture.

7. Pipe the soufflé mixture into the ramekins. Smooth the tops and then gently run your fingertip around the edge of the ramekins (so the batter loosens and rises properly in the oven). Bake on the lower rack of the oven for 10–12 minutes, until soufflés are browned, puffed, and still slightly wobbly. Serve immediately.

pistachio meringues

Makes about 60

½ cup (50 g) shelled pistachios, divided
1 recipe Swiss Meringue (page 37)

Special equipment: food processor, piping bag(s) fitted with nozzle tip(s)

1. Preheat the oven to 220°F (105°C). Line 2 baking sheets with parchment paper or silicone baking mats.
2. Using the food processor, grind ¼ cup (25 g) of the pistachios into a fine flour.
3. Fold the ground pistachios into the meringue mixture. Chop the remaining pistachios and reserve.
4. Fill the piping bag(s) with the mixture.
5. Pipe the meringue onto the baking sheets into rounds about 1 ¼ inches (3 cm) in diameter.
6. Sprinkle the remaining pistachios over the top of the meringues and bake in the middle of the oven for about 50-60 minutes, until the meringues can be easily lifted off the sheet. Remove and let cool.

Tip: Almond meringues or hazelnut meringues are also delicious—use the same recipe but swap out the nuts. For almond meringues, a dash of almond extract can enhance the flavor.

chocolate meringues

Makes about 60

2 ¾ ounces (80 g) 70% dark chocolate, chopped
1 recipe Swiss Meringue (page 37)

1. Preheat the oven to 220°F (105°C). Line 2 baking sheets with parchment paper or silicone baking mats.
2. Melt the chocolate in a heatproof bowl set over a pot of simmering water. Let the chocolate cool slightly.
3. Gently fold the melted chocolate into the meringue mixture, ensuring that the chocolate doesn't mix in completely but forms large swirls throughout.
4. Using a couple of spoons, drop the mixture onto the baking sheets in dollops about 1 ¼ inches (3 cm) in diameter.
5. Bake in the middle of the oven for about 50-60 minutes, until the meringues can be easily lifted off the tray. Remove and let cool.

berry meringues

Makes about 60

4 tablespoons freeze-dried berry powder, such as raspberry, blackberry, blueberry, or strawberry
1 batch Swiss Meringue (page 37)
Special equipment: piping bag(s) fitted with nozzle tip(s), clean thin paintbrush

1. Preheat the oven to 220°F (105°C). Line 2 baking sheets with parchment paper or silicone baking mats.
2. In a small bowl, mix the berry powder and 3 tablespoons water into a paste.
3. Use the paintbrush to paint 4–5 vertical stripes of the berry paste on the inside of the piping bags.
4. Gently fill the bags with meringue and pipe the meringue onto the baking sheets into rounds about 1 ¼ inches (3 cm) in diameter.
5. Bake in the middle of the oven for about 50–60 minutes, until the meringues can be easily lifted off the tray. Remove and let cool.

Tip: Berry powder is made from freeze-dried berries and can be found in well-stocked food stores or spice shops. If you can't find the powder, blend freeze-dried berries into a powder using a blender. Alternatively, you can pipe plain meringue and sprinkle berry powder on top before baking.

sabayon

It's hard to believe that this heavenly dessert is made with only three simple ingredients. If you're familiar with Italian zabaglione, this is the French version.

Makes 4 servings

3 ⅓ tablespoons granulated sugar
4 egg yolks
Scant ½ cup (about 110 ml) Marsala wine
Assorted fresh berries

1. In a large stainless steel bowl with a rounded bottom, whisk together the sugar, egg yolks, and Marsala.
2. Place the bowl over simmering water and whisk vigorously for about 10 minutes, until a fluffy cream forms.
3. Remove from heat and whisk for another minute.
4. Serve the cream in dishes, topped with the berries.

Tip: For a more elevated dessert, berries and sabayon can be briefly cooked under a broiler, which turns the sabayon a golden brown and adds caramelization. Place berries in a greased heatproof dish, top with sabayon, and place under a broiler for about 5 minutes, keeping a close eye on it to make sure it doesn't burn.

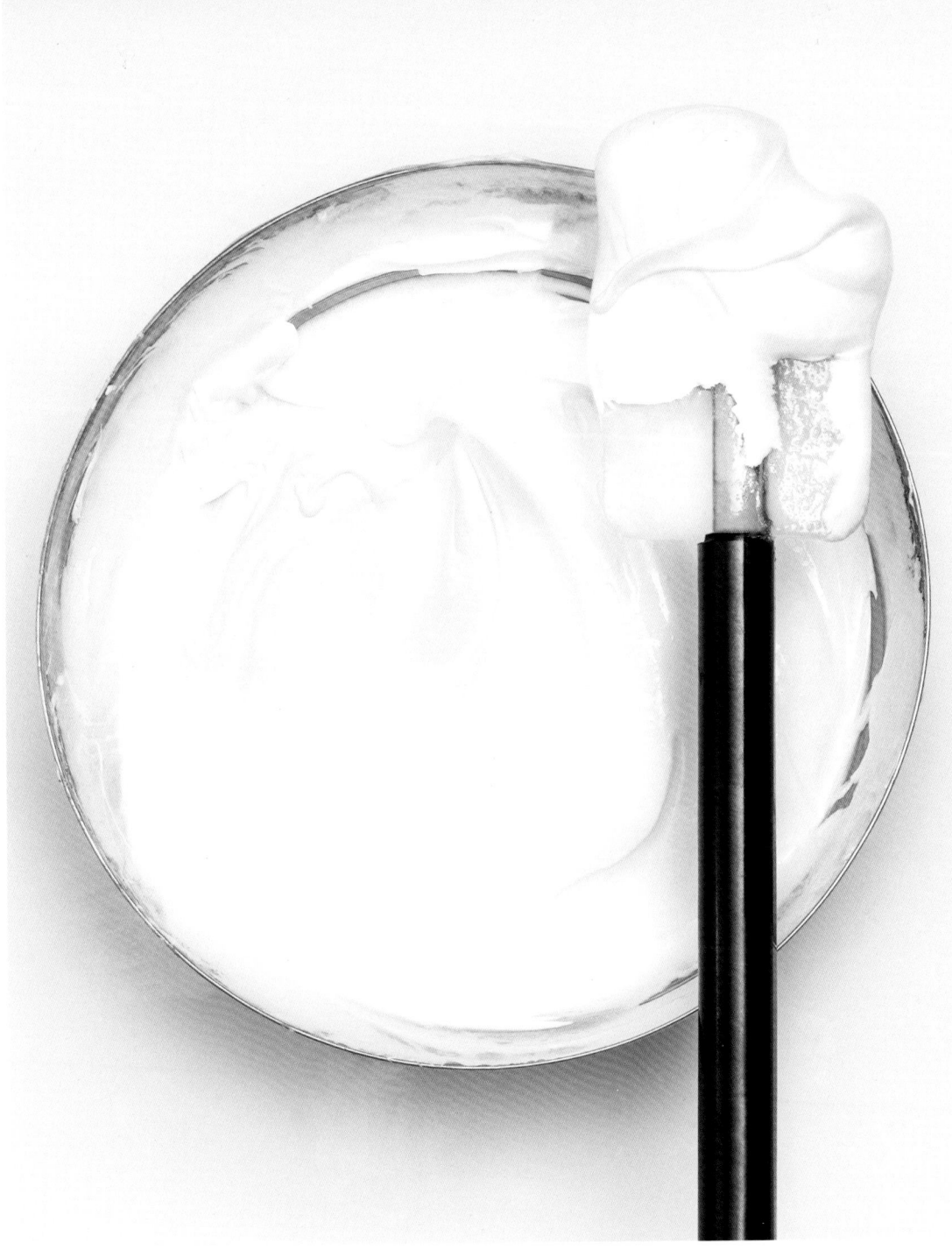

Other Delicious Meringue Flavors

Fennel seeds/anise and finely grated lemon zest · Crumbled dried rose petals · Cinnamon and finely grated orange zest · Licorice powder · Peppermint oil · Absinthe or amaretto liqueur

raspberry marshmallows

Making marshmallows is sticky business. Sometimes I rub a little oil on my hands when pressing the marshmallows into the mold. Almost anything works as a marshmallow flavoring—lemon, peppermint oil, various berry powders, sesame seeds, roasted nuts, licorice powder, toasted coconut, cocoa, or even herbs.

Makes about 36 marshmallows

3 envelopes (about 6 ¼ teaspoons/21 g) unflavored powdered gelatin

½ cup (120 ml) cold water

2 cups (400 g) granulated sugar

3 tablespoons glucose syrup

2 egg whites

3 tablespoons freeze-dried raspberry powder, divided

Scraped seeds from ½ vanilla bean

3 tablespoons plus 1 teaspoon powdered sugar

3 tablespoons plus 1 teaspoon cornstarch

Special equipment: candy thermometer, hand mixer or stand mixer fitted with the whisk attachment, 12 x 12-inch (30 x 30-cm) baking pan

1. Sprinkle the gelatin over the cold water and let it bloom for 5–10 minutes.

2. In a saucepan, combine ¾ cup (180 ml) water with the sugar and glucose syrup. Bring to a boil and cook, checking with the thermometer, until the mixture reaches 284°F (140°C). Remove from heat.

3. Using the hand mixer or stand mixer, whip the egg whites to soft peaks. Add 2 tablespoons of the raspberry powder and the vanilla seeds, and keep whipping.

4. Add the hot sugar syrup in a thin stream, whipping constantly. Continue whipping until the mixture cools to about 104°F (40°C).

5. Add the bloomed gelatin to the meringue mixture, and whip for about 3 more minutes, until the mixture is firm and slightly sticky.

6. In a medium bowl, combine the powdered sugar and cornstarch. Dust the baking pan with half the mixture.

7. Pour the mixture into the prepared pan and smooth the surface with an offset spatula or knife. Dust lightly with the remaining powdered sugar mixture. Sprinkle with the remaining 1 tablespoon of raspberry powder.

8. Cover and let sit at room temperature for 1 day.

9. Cut into 2-inch (5-cm) cubes and, if desired, roll in additional powdered sugar and cornstarch.

Tip: You can find glucose syrup online or in well-stocked grocery stores. While corn syrup is similar, it has a different water content so it's not a perfect substitute.

candied egg yolk with almond meringue

Makes 4 servings

Candied Egg Yolk

1 tablespoon dried lavender

1 ¼ cups (250 g) granulated sugar, divided

4 egg yolks

Almond Meringue

Scant ½ cup (about 50 g) almond flour

¼ teaspoon almond extract

½ recipe Swiss Meringue (page 37)

Ice Cream

Scant ½ cup (about 150 g) sweetened condensed milk

3 ⅓ tablespoons glucose syrup

3 ½ ounces (100 g) cream cheese, at room temperature

¾ cup (175 g) Greek yogurt

Granulated sugar, for serving

4 tablespoons finely chopped pistachios, for garnish

Special equipment: tea strainer, piping bag, ice cream maker, cooking blowtorch

Candied Egg Yolk

1. Place the lavender in a tea strainer. In a small saucepan, combine ¾ cup (180 ml) water and ¾ cup (150 g) of the sugar. Insert the tea strainer into the liquid, and bring to a boil. Let cool to room temperature.

2. Remove the strainer and pour the lavender syrup into a small jar with a lid. Carefully add the egg yolks.

3. Sprinkle with the remaining sugar, cover, and refrigerate for 3 days.

Meringue

4. Preheat the oven to 220°F (105°C). Line a baking sheet with parchment paper or a silicone baking mat.

5. Fold the almond flour and almond extract into the meringue.

6. Fill the piping bag with meringue and pipe the meringue into 10 rounds on the baking sheet.

7. Bake in the middle of the oven for about 50–60 minutes, until the meringues can be easily lifted off the tray. Remove and let cool. Reserve 4 meringues for serving and set the rest aside for another use.

Ice Cream

8. In a large bowl, whisk together the condensed milk, glucose syrup, cream cheese, and yogurt. Churn in the ice cream maker until creamy. (Ideally, the ice cream will be ready just before serving the dish, so you can serve it straight from the churner and avoid having to put it in the freezer. If not, allow the ice cream to soften briefly before serving.)

9. To plate and serve, gently lift the egg yolks from the syrup and place each one on a plate. Sprinkle the yolks with granulated sugar and use the blowtorch to caramelize the tops. Place 1 almond meringue on each of 4 plates. Top each meringue with a caramelized yolk. Add a scoop of ice cream to each plate and garnish with chopped pistachios.

Tip: You can find glucose syrup online or in well-stocked grocery stores. While corn syrup is similar, it has different water content so it's not a perfect substitute.

The first time I had candied egg yolk was at Le Chateaubriand in Paris. It was 2 a.m. after a long tasting menu. The restaurant was loud, there had been many glasses of wine, I was a bit sleepy, and a French waiter served me the dish without any preamble. I thought I was digging into a candied apricot, so imagine my surprise when I tasted sweet egg yolk instead. Since that time, I've tried candied egg yolk multiple times. Sometimes the yolks are infused with herbs like rosemary or lavender, and when the top is caramelized, à la crème brûlée, the treat reaches the peak of dessert satisfaction.

In this recipe, I've combined a small almond meringue with lavender-candied egg yolk, yogurt-and-condensed-milk ice cream, and pistachios to create my own interpretation of this now-world-famous dessert.

Île Flottante, a poached meringue floating in vanilla sauce topped with caramel, may sound incredibly sweet—and most of the time, when you're served this classic in France, it is just that. My version is based on a classic crème anglaise, but at the end, I add a generous amount of lemon juice to balance the vanilla and sweetness with a refreshing tang. Served in small portions, it's absolutely delicious.

île flottante

Makes 2-6 servings

3 ⅓ tablespoons granulated sugar
Pinch of salt
1 recipe Crème Anglaise (below)
4 tablespoons freshly squeezed lemon juice
½ recipe Classic Cold-Whipped Meringue (page 35)

1. Make the caramel: In a small saucepan over medium heat, combine the sugar, 1 ½ tablespoons water, and a pinch of salt, and stir until golden. Pour onto a baking sheet lined with parchment paper or a silicone baking mat and let cool. Once cool, chop finely.
2. Place the crème anglaise in a bowl and stir in the lemon juice. Chill before serving.
3. Fill a large saucepan with water and bring to a simmer. Take large spoonfuls of meringue and gently place in the simmering water; poach, turning once, for about 5 minutes, or until set.
4. To serve, place the crème anglaise in bowls and top with poached meringue. Sprinkle with the chopped caramel.

crème anglaise

Makes about 2 cups (500 ml) of sauce

1 cup (240 ml) whole milk
1 cup (240 ml) heavy cream
Scraped seeds from ½ vanilla bean
6 egg yolks
⅓ cup (65 g) granulated sugar
Special equipment: candy thermometer (optional)

1. In a large saucepan, combine the milk, cream, and vanilla seeds. Bring to a boil, then turn off the heat and let cool slightly.
2. In a large bowl, whisk together the egg yolks and sugar. Gradually whisk in the hot milk and cream mixture.
3. Pour the mixture back into the saucepan and gently heat until it thickens but is still runny and the temperature reaches 185°F (85°C). Don't let it go any higher, otherwise it will turn into scrambled eggs. (If you don't have a thermometer, you can use the "spoon test": Stir the sauce with a wooden spoon, and when it starts to thicken slightly, pull the spoon out and use your finger to draw a line across the back of the spoon. If the line remains, the sauce is thick enough.)
4. Pour into a clean, heatproof bowl and let it cool slightly. Cover with plastic wrap, ensuring the wrap touches the surface of the sauce to prevent a skin from forming.
5. Let the crème anglaise cool completely and then refrigerate in an airtight container until ready to serve for up to 5 days.

crème brûlée

This decadent dessert is always a crowd-pleaser—and it's also easy to make.

Makes 4-6 servings

1 ¼ cups (300 ml) heavy cream
¾ cup (180 ml) whole milk
Scraped seeds from 1 vanilla bean
Salt
6 egg yolks
Scant ½ cup (about 90 g) granulated sugar
Scant ½ cup (about 100 g) raw sugar

Special equipment: 4-6 small ramekins or crème brûlée molds, large, high-sided baking pan big enough to hold all the ramekins, food processor or mortar and pestle, cooking blowtorch

1. Preheat the oven to 250°F (120°C). Place the baking pan into the center of the oven. Use a pitcher to pour water into the pan until it comes halfway up the sides.
2. In a large saucepan, combine the cream, milk, vanilla seeds, and a pinch of salt, and bring to a boil. Remove from the heat and let cool slightly.
3. In a large, heatproof bowl, whisk together the egg yolks and granulated sugar. Very gradually whisk the hot cream mixture into the egg yolks.
4. Pour the mixture into the ramekins or crème brûlée molds.
5. Place the molds in the water bath in the oven and bake for about 1 hour, until the custard is set but still slightly jiggly.
6. Let cool to room temperature, then refrigerate until serving.
7. Grind the raw sugar to a fine powder using the food processor or mortar and pestle.
8. Sprinkle a thin layer of raw sugar over the top of the baked crème brûlées and use the blowtorch to caramelize the sugar. If desired, add more sugar and caramelize again for a thicker, crispier caramelized layer. (The brûlée tastes best when it's double-caramelized, creating a thicker layer of sugar that forms a hard, crisp shell over the smooth vanilla cream.)

Steamed Brûlée?

Just like *chawanmushi* (page 178), you can steam crème brûlée for a delightful result. While the classic method is to bake it in the oven in a water bath, steaming is faster and produces a firm yet fluffy custard.

sweets & cocktails

caramel pots de crème

This dessert is like a caramel crème brûlée without the caramelized sugar crust. Pot de crème can be made in several flavors, with vanilla and chocolate being especially common in France.

Makes 6 servings

½ cup plus 2 tablespoons granulated sugar, divided
¾ cup (180 ml) heavy cream
¾ cup (180 ml) whole milk
Scraped seeds from ½ vanilla bean
5 egg yolks
Whipped cream, for serving
Cocoa powder, for serving

Special equipment: 6 small ramekins or glass jars

1. In a small saucepan over medium heat, combine a scant ½ cup of the sugar and 1 tablespoon water. Do not stir; allow the sugar to caramelize and turn golden brown, swirling the saucepan if necessary for even browning.
2. Remove from heat, and slowly stir in the cream and milk. Return to low heat, and stir until a smooth sauce forms.
3. Remove from heat and let cool.
4. Preheat the oven to 300°F (150°C).
5. In a large bowl, whisk together the vanilla seeds, egg yolks, and the remaining sugar. Whisk in the cooled caramel sauce.
6. Pour the mixture into the glass jars or ramekins and cover each one with foil. Place the jars in a deep baking dish and fill with hot water nearly to the tops of the jars.
7. Bake in the center of the oven for 35–40 minutes. Let cool and store in the refrigerator until set, about 3 hours.
8. Top each pot de crème with whipped cream and a dusting of cocoa powder.

crème caramel

Unlike crème brûlée, crème caramel is made with milk instead of cream. For me, it's best served cold straight from the refrigerator, with the burnt caramel sauce running around the wobbly egg custard. Take it out of the oven when it still jiggles in the center—if baked too long, the dessert ends up tasting like baked eggs.

Makes 4-6 servings

2 cups (480 ml) whole milk
1 cup (200 g) granulated sugar, divided
1 vanilla bean, sliced lengthwise
Peel of ½ lemon, cut into thick strips
3 eggs, beaten

Special equipment: candy thermometer, ramekins or crème brûlée molds, large, high-sided baking pan big enough to hold all the ramekins

1. Preheat the oven to 255°F (125°C) and place an ovenproof dish of water in the center of the oven.

2. In a large saucepan, combine the milk and ⅓ cup (65 g) of the sugar. Scrape the seeds from the vanilla bean into the milk, and drop in the scraped bean halves. Bring to a boil, then remove from heat and let cool slightly. Remove the vanilla bean halves.

3. In a small saucepan over medium heat, combine the remaining sugar with 2 tablespoons of water. Do not stir; allow the sugar to caramelize and turn golden brown, swirling the saucepan if necessary for even browning.

4. Remove from heat and stir in the lemon peel. Carefully stir in a scant ½ cup (115 ml) water (it may splatter).

5. Return the saucepan to medium heat and let the mixture cook into a thick caramel sauce until it reaches 250°F (121°C).

6. Remove the lemon peel and pour the hot caramel into the ramekins or brûlée molds. Let the caramel cool in the molds.

7. Stir the eggs into the milk mixture, and pour into the molds over the caramel.

8. Cover the molds with aluminum foil and place them in the water bath.

9. Bake in the center of the oven for 1-1 ½ hours, depending on the portion size, until custard is set with a slight wobble in the center.

10. Remove and let cool to room temperature. Chill at least 3 hours.

11. To serve, loosen the edges of the custard with a small paring knife. Invert the molds onto plates so the caramel sauce flows around the pudding.

Tip: Crème caramel and flan are essentially the same dessert: both are egg-based custards topped with a caramel sauce. The term "crème caramel" is common in France (and other parts of Europe), whereas "flan" is more commonly used in Spain, Latin America, and the US.

sweets & cocktails

purin

This sweet egg custard is Japan's answer to crème caramel, and a sign of Western influence on the country's cuisine. *Purin* is the Japanese word for "pudding."

Makes 4 servings

Caramel

Scant ½ cup (about 90 g) granulated sugar

Custard

1 ⅔ cups (400 ml) whole milk

3 eggs

⅓ cup (65 g) granulated sugar

¼ teaspoon scraped seeds from a vanilla bean

Special equipment: 4 ramekins or crème brûlée molds

1. Make the caramel: In a small saucepan over medium heat, combine the sugar and 3 ⅓ tablespoons of water. Do not stir; allow the sugar to caramelize and turn golden brown, swirling the saucepan if necessary for even browning.
2. Pour into the ramekins or crème brûlée molds.
3. Make the custard: In a medium saucepan over medium heat, warm the milk gently. Let cool slightly. In a medium bowl, whisk together the eggs, sugar, and vanilla seeds. Gradually whisk the milk into the egg mixture.
4. Strain the mixture through a fine sieve.
5. Pour the strained mixture over the caramel sauce in the molds. Cover each mold with plastic wrap.
6. Place the molds in a deep saucepan with high sides. Fill with warm water until it reaches ¾ up the sides of the molds.
7. Cover the saucepan with foil and bring the water to a boil, then reduce the heat to low and simmer for 5 minutes.
8. Turn off the heat and let stand for 10 minutes.
9. Remove the molds from water and let cool at room temperature, then refrigerate for at least 3 hours and preferably overnight.
10. To serve, invert the molds onto plates so the caramel sauce flows around the pudding.

egg cocktails

Eggs can give cocktails a soft, fluffy, and creamy texture that nothing else can replicate. Whole eggs are used in flips, liqueurs, or eggnog, while egg whites star in drinks like fizzes or sours.

Shaking egg whites into a cocktail can be a bit tricky because citrus, a common cocktail ingredient, can cause the liquid to separate from the egg. The acidity makes the egg coagulate, so it's crucial to shake the drink thoroughly to create an even foam. The goal is to get all the ingredients to blend smoothly into one cohesive mixture.

When making an egg white cocktail, it should always be dry shaken (shaken without ice). This allows the proteins to spread out and create a smooth, soft foam. If you add ice from the start, the proteins will be compressed by the cold.

Only after you've dry shaken should you add ice to chill the liquid—just don't shake for too long, as the ice will melt and dilute the mixture. Too much water will also reduce the volume of the fluffy egg white. If this sounds like a lot of rules, don't worry; you'll quickly get the hang of it.

simple syrup

Many cocktails call for simple syrup. It's handy to make a large batch because it keeps indefinitely in the refrigerator.

Makes about 1 ¼ cups (310 ml)

1 ¼ cups (250 g) granulated sugar

1. In a medium saucepan, combine sugar and 1 ¼ cups (300 ml) water and bring to a boil.
2. Reduce the heat to low and simmer until the sugar is fully dissolved, stirring occasionally.
3. Let cool and store in a lidded jar in the refrigerator.

pisco sour

Pisco is a grape brandy with Peruvian and Chilean roots. My version of the cocktail incorporates Angostura bitters into the drink itself, but a more traditional take is adding the bitters as a garnish.

Makes 1 cocktail

1 ⅓ ounces (40 ml) freshly squeezed lime juice
1 ounce (30 ml) simple syrup
2 ounces (60 ml) pisco
Orange or Angostura bitters
1 egg white
Ice

Special equipment: cocktail shaker

1. In the cocktail shaker, combine the lime juice, simple syrup, pisco, 2 dashes of the bitters, and the egg white.
2. Shake for 60 seconds until a foamy layer forms.
3. Open the shaker and add ice. Shake again until the drink is cold. Do not over-shake, as too much water will dilute the drink.
4. Strain into a glass.

sweets & cocktails

ramos gin fizz

This cocktail is all about pomp and circumstance. The original recipe, which hails from New Orleans in the 1880s, was shaken for up to 15 minutes and yielded a glorious, fluffy head. This version is far less laborious but no less delicious.

Makes 1 cocktail

2 ounces (60 ml) gin
1 ounce (30 ml) freshly squeezed lemon juice
1 ounce (30 ml) simple syrup
2 ounces (60 ml) heavy cream
1 egg white
2 dashes orange blossom water
Ice
3 ⅓ ounces (100 ml) soda water

Special equipment:
cocktail shaker

1. In the cocktail shaker, combine the gin, lemon juice, simple syrup, cream, egg white, and orange blossom water.
2. Shake for about 30 seconds to create foam from the mixing of the cream and egg white.
3. Fill the shaker with ice and shake until the drink is very cold, smooth, and foamy. It may take a good bit of shaking!
4. Strain into a tall glass and top with soda water.

salty mezcal cucumber sour

Makes 1 cocktail

1 lemon wedge, for rimming
Salt, for rimming
5 slices cucumber
⅔ ounce (20 ml) pisco
⅔ ounce (20 ml) mezcal
⅔ ounce (20 ml) freshly squeezed lemon juice
⅔ ounce (20 ml) simple syrup
1 egg white
Ice
Angostura bitters
Special equipment: muddler, cocktail shaker

1. Rub the lemon wedge around the rim of a cocktail glass. Dip the rim in salt.
2. Muddle cucumber in the bottom of the shaker. Add the pisco, mezcal, lemon juice, simple syrup, and egg white.
3. Shake for about 30 seconds to form a fluffy egg white foam.
4. Open the shaker and add ice. Shake until the drink is cold.
5. Strain into the glass and top with a few dashes of bitters.

sweets & cocktails

clover club

Makes 1 cocktail

Scant ½ cup (about 90 g) granulated sugar

3 ⅓ tablespoons fresh or frozen raspberries

1 ounce (30 ml) freshly squeezed lemon juice

2 ounces (60 ml) gin

1 egg white

Ice

Special equipment: cocktail shaker

1. Make a raspberry simple syrup by combining 3 ⅓ tablespoons water with the sugar and raspberries in a small saucepan. Bring to a boil, stirring to crush the raspberries and dissolve the sugar. Let cool, then strain through a fine sieve. Measure out 1 ounce (30 ml) of the syrup and set remaining syrup aside for topping.
2. In the cocktail shaker, combine the raspberry syrup, lemon juice, gin, and egg white. Shake for up to 60 seconds until foamy.
3. Open the shaker and fill with ice. Shake until cold.
4. Strain into a glass and top with extra syrup.

eggnog

sweets & cocktails

eggnog

This decadent cocktail is popular during the holidays when big punch bowls are laid out and revelers serve themselves. Note that this recipe is for a single serving. If you're making it for a party, this recipe is designed to be multiplied. However, it includes whipped egg whites that can deflate, so don't let it sit too long before serving.

Makes 1 serving

1 egg
1 ½ tablespoons granulated sugar, divided
2 tablespoons whole milk
2 tablespoons heavy cream
1 ¾ ounces (50 ml) dark rum or brandy
Freshly grated nutmeg

1. Separate the egg white and yolk into two separate small bowls.
2. Whisk the yolk with 1 tablespoon of the sugar until pale and fluffy. Add the milk, cream, rum (or brandy), and a pinch of nutmeg.
3. Whip the egg white into soft peaks. Gradually whisk in the remaining ½ tablespoon of sugar until stiff peaks form, creating a firm meringue.
4. Gently fold the meringue into the yolk mixture. Pour into a glass and serve immediately.

Tip: Try experimenting with different flavors by replacing the rum or brandy with Cointreau or amaretto. Adding amaretto and cocoa powder tastes like a liquid tiramisu–delicious.

egg liqueur

This European liqueur is similar to eggnog, but uses vodka in addition to rum or brandy and swaps in sweetened condensed milk for whole milk.

Makes about 2 cups (480 ml)

¾ cup (180 ml) heavy cream
1 vanilla bean, cut in half horizontally
Peel of ½ orange, cut into thick strips
5 egg yolks
⅔ cup (80 g) powdered sugar
Scant ½ cup (about 120 ml) condensed milk
Scant ½ cup (about 120 ml) vodka
3 ⅓ tablespoons rum or brandy

1. In a medium saucepan over medium heat, combine the cream, one vanilla bean half (save the other half for another use), and orange peel.
2. Bring to just below a simmer, then cool and strain.
3. In a medium bowl, whisk the egg yolks and powdered sugar into a fluffy mixture. Add the cooled cream, condensed milk, vodka, and brandy or rum.
4. Pour into a clean glass bottle and store in the refrigerator for up to 1 week.

index

0-9

3- to 11-Minute Eggs - p. 10
63-Degree Eggs - p. 32
63-Degree Egg with Vendace Roe & Broccoli Cream - p. 103
64-Degree Eggs - p. 32
65-Degree Eggs - p. 32

a

Aioli - p. 39
American-Style Whole-Egg Mayonnaise - p. 39
Asian Beef Tartare with Gochujang Mayonnaise - p. 116
Avocado-Baked Egg - p. 96

b

Bánh Xèo - p. 158
Béarnaise - p. 40
Berry Meringues - p. 200
Berry Soufflé - p. 194
Bibimbap - p. 157
Black Pudding Scotch Egg - p. 84
Boiled Eggs & Soldiers - p. 59
Breakfast Burrito - p. 52
Brioche - p. 61
Brown Sauce HP-Style - p. 78
Burger with Egg, Avocado & Sriracha Mayo - p. 150
Butter-Fried Egg - p. 15

c

Caesar Dressing - p. 41
Candied Egg Yolk with Almond Meringue - p. 204
Caramel Pots de Crème - p. 210
Carbonara - p. 139
Chashu Pork - p. 167
Chawanmushi - p. 178
Chicken Egg Soup with Black Rice - p. 154
Chinese Tea Eggs - p. 89
Chocolate Meringues - p. 199
Chocolate Soufflé with Sea Salt - p. 197
Chorizo Scotch Egg - p. 84
Choron, Sauce - p. 40
Classic Cold-Whipped Meringue - p. 35
Classic French Fried Egg - p. 14
Classic French Omelet - p. 26
Classic Scotch Egg - p. 83
Clover Club - p. 219
Cocktails
   Clover Club - p. 219
   Eggnog - p. 221
   Egg Liqueur - p. 221
   Pisco Sour - p. 216
   Ramos Gin Fizz - p. 217
   Salty Mezcal Cucumber Sour - p. 218
Cocottes
   Eggs en Cocotte with Spinach - p. 99
   Eggs en Cocotte with Tomato - p. 99
Crème Anglaise - p. 207
Crème Brûlée - p. 209
Crème Caramel - p. 213
Crispy Fried Egg - p. 16
Croque Madame - p. 53
Crunchy Chili Oil - p. 75
Custard Pie - p. 190

d

Dan Tat - p. 193
Deviled Eggs - p. 92
Dukkah - p. 21

e

Eggnog - p. 221
Egg & Tomato with Crunchy Chili Oil - p. 75
Egg & Anchovy Salad - p. 133
Egg Muffin - p. 49
Egg Liqueur - p. 221
Egg Pasta - p. 139
Egg Ramen Noodles - p. 161
Egg Sandwiches & Toasts
   Crispbread with Egg, Potato & Sandwich Caviar - p. 72
   Egg & Avocado Toast - p. 68
   Egg & Mayo Toast - p. 73
   Egg & Tomato Levain Toast - p. 68
   Egg & Tunacado Toast - p. 73
   Egg in a Basket - p. 69
   Egg Sandwich - p. 56
   Open-Faced Rye Sandwich with Egg & Anchovies - p. 72
   Soft Rye Toast with Egg & Swedish Sausage - p. 69

index

Eggs Benedict - p. 62
Eggs Benedict with Mushroom & Fennel Hollandaise - p. 64
Eggs Benedict with Salmon & Dill-Horseradish Hollandaise - p. 65
Eggs Florentine - p. 62
English Muffin - p. 49

f

French Farmer's Omelet - p. 28
Fried Eggs
    Crispy Fried Egg - p. 16
    Classic French Fried Egg - p. 14
    Butter-Fried Egg - p. 15
Frittata, Italian - p. 129
Full English Breakfast - p. 46

g

Gribiche, Sauce - p. 41

h

Herb Mayonnaise - p. 40
Hollandaise - p. 39
Homemade Ketchup - p. 79
Homemade Mustard - p. 79
Huevos Rancheros - p. 50

i

Île Flottante - p. 207
Italian Frittata - p. 129
Italian Meringue - p. 36
Italian Steak Tartare - p. 115

j

Jianbing - p. 76

k

Ketchup, Homemade - p. 79
Kimchi Ramen with 64-Degree Egg - p. 165
Kimchi Udon & Egg - p. 171

l

Lyonnaise Salad - p. 135

m

Mayonnaise
    American-Style Whole-Egg Mayonnaise - p. 39
    Soy Mayonnaise - p. 41
    Herb Mayonnaise - p. 40
    Mayonnaise & Aioli - p. 39
Marshmallows, Raspberry - p. 203
Meringue
    Berry Meringues - p. 200
    Chocolate Meringues - p. 199
    Classic Cold-Whipped Meringue - p. 35
    Italian Meringue - p. 38
    Pistachio Meringues - p. 199
    Swiss Meringue - p. 37
Miso & Sesame Ramen - p. 166

n

Niçoise Salad - p. 130
Nobis Dressing - p. 40
Noisette, Sauce - p. 39
Noodles, Egg Ramen - p. 161

o

Omelet
    Classic French Omelet - p. 26
    French Farmer's Omelet - p. 28
    Tamagoyaki - p. 30
Oto - p. 175
Oyakodon - p. 178

p

Parisian Sandwich - p. 123
Party Eggs with Shrimp & Roe - p. 93
Pasta with Sausage & Egg - p. 141
Pasta, Egg - p. 139
Pastéis de Nata - p. 188
Pickled Beetroot Egg - p. 90
Pickled Dill Egg - p. 91
Pickled Herring with 65-Degree Eggs & Browned Butter - p. 149
Pisco Sour - p. 216
Pistachio Meringues - p. 199
Pizza Bianca with Pancetta & Radicchio - p. 184
Pizza Dough - p. 182
Pizza with Chorizo & Spinach - p. 185
Poached Eggs, Classic - p. 18
Poached Eggs, Rookie - p. 19

index

Poached Quail Eggs - p. 20
Polenta with Mushrooms & Egg - p. 145
Potato Curry Scotch Egg - p. 85
Purin - p. 214

Radishes with Soft-Boiled Egg & Five-Spice Pork, Warm - p. 100
Ramen
    Egg Ramen Noodles - p. 161
    Kimchi Ramen with 64-Degree Egg - p. 165
    Miso & Sesame Ramen - p. 166
    Shio Tofu Ramen - p. 167
Ramen Broth - p. 162
Ramos Gin Fizz - p. 217
Raspberry Marshmallows - p. 203
Ravioli with Ricotta & Quail Eggs - p. 142
Rillettes, Salmon with Poached Quail Eggs - p. 95

Sabayon - p. 200
Salad, Lyonnaise - p. 135
Salad, Niçoise - p. 130
Salmon Rillettes with Poached Quail Eggs - p. 95
Salty Mezcal Cucumber Sour - p. 218
Sauces
    Béarnaise - p. 40
    Brown Sauce HP-Style - p. 78
    Choron - p. 40
    Gribiche - p. 41
    Hollandaise - p. 39
    Noisette - p. 39

Scrambled Eggs in a Frying Pan - p. 22
Scrambled Eggs Cooked Over a Water Bath - p. 23
Scotch Eggs
    Black Pudding Scotch Egg - p. 84
    Classic Scotch Egg - p. 83
    Chorizo Scotch Egg - p. 84
    Potato Curry Scotch Egg - p. 85
Shakshuka - p. 67
Shio Tofu Ramen - p. 167
"Son-in-Law" Thai Eggs - p. 172
Soufflés
    Apple & Nut Soufflé - p. 196
    Berry Soufflé - p. 194
    Chocolate Soufflé with Sea Salt - p. 197
Soy Mayonnaise - p. 41
Spanish Tortilla - p. 129
Steak Hash - p. 146
Swedish Beef & Potatoes - p. 126
Swedish "Dutch Baby" with Pork - p. 108
Swedish Steak Tartare - p. 111
Swedish Toast with Tenderloin, Roe, and Egg - p. 119
Swiss Meringue - p. 37

t

Tamagoyaki - p. 30
Tartares
    Asian Beef Tartare with Gochujang Mayonnaise - p. 116
    Egg and Anchovy Tartare - p. 133
    Italian Steak Tartare - p. 115
    Steak Tartare with Confit Egg Yolk - p. 112

Swedish Steak Tartare - p. 111
Veal Tartare with Tarragon, Anchovy Mayo, and Fried Capers - p. 120
Tarts
    Dan Tat - p. 193
    Pastéis de nata - p. 188
Tea Eggs, Chinese - p. 89
Thai Eggs, "Son-in-Law" - p. 172
Toasts
    Crispbread with Egg, Potato & Caviar - p. 72
    Egg & Avocado Toast - p. 68
    Egg & Mayo Toast - p. 73
    Egg & Tomato Levain Toast - p. 68
    Egg & Tunacado Toast - p. 73
    Egg in a Basket - p. 69
    Open-Faced Rye Sandwich with Egg & Anchovies - p. 72
    Soft Rye Toast with Egg & Swedish Sausage - p. 69
Torta Pasqualina - p. 180
Tsukune - p. 179

v

Veal Tartare with Tarragon, Anchovy Mayo, and Fried Capers - p. 120
Vietnamese Salad with Egg - p. 153

w

Warm Radishes with Soft-Boiled Egg & Five-Spice Pork - p. 100

Eggs: All Day, Every Way
Tove Nilsson

Photography by
Charlie Drevstam

Design by
Scott McNally

U.S. Edition
Publisher and Creative Director
Ilona Oppenheim

Art and Design Director
Jefferson Quintana

Editorial Director
Lisa McGuinness

Tra Eats Editor
Amanda M. Faison

Publishing Director
Jessica Faroy

Senior Designer
Morgane Leoni

Proofreader
Robin Miller

This product is made of FSC ®-certified and other controlled material. Tra Publishing is committed to sustainability in its materials and practices.

Printed and bound in China by Artron Art Co., Ltd.

Title was first published in the United States by Tra Publishing in 2026.

© 2022 Tove Nilsson

First published in 2022 by Natur & Kultur, Sweden under the original title *Ägg*.

No part of this book may be reproduced or transmitted in any form or by any means (electronic or mechanical, including photocopying, recording or any information retrieval system) without permission in writing from the publisher.

ISBN: 978-1-962098-33-5

Tra Publishing
245 NE 37th Street
Miami, FL 33137
trapublishing.com

1 2 3 4 5 6 7 8 9 10